A Culture of Kindness

For leaders of the future

Nahla Summers

ISBN-9781086023664:

Contents

Kindness
noun

The quality of being friendly, generous and considerate

'he thanked them for their kindness and support'
synonyms: kindliness, kind-heartedness, warm-heartedness, tender-heartedness, goodwill, affectionateness, affection, warmth, gentleness, tenderness, concern, care.

Kindness is a behaviour marked by ethical characteristics, a pleasant disposition, and concern and consideration for others. It is considered a virtue, and is recognised as a value in many cultures and religions (see ethics in religion).
(Oxford Dictionary)

Culture
noun

Culture (/ˈkʌltʃər/) is the social behavior and norms found in human societies.

Culture is considered a central concept in anthropology, encompassing the range of phenomena that are transmitted through social learning in human societies.
(Oxford Dictionary)

Ultimately, culture is simply a way of life.

Foreword

Profitable, powerful, productive... these are all words we use to describe leaders, yet we so rarely mention or celebrate kindness. Indeed, too often we associate kindness with weakness - but nothing could be further from the truth.

As the Founder of the Women of the Future Programme, a range of platforms and initiatives which celebrate some of the most successful women all over the world, I have seen the true power of kindness in business and leadership.

Nahla Summers' book *A Culture of Kindness* resonates with my belief that kindness should lie at the heart of leadership. It is a practical guide to how kindness can be introduced into the workplace with the values of gratitude, empathy, integrity, honesty and trust, values which we need to ensure are embedded into the DNA of leadership.

This book provides a perfect road map on a subject that is more important than ever before. It is no easy task to move kindness to centre stage, in our divisive, polarised and discordant world. Yet this is exactly what the author does, with examples and practical tips. Whilst we often read about random acts of kindness, I think we also need to be purposefully kind as well. Try being kind, because nothing can make your life more magical than perpetual kindness.

Pinky Lilani CBE DL
Founder and Chairman, Women of the Future Programme

Preface

I have changed the lens in which I see the world and to be kind is the only possible result.

Benjamin Mathes, Founder, Urban Confessional

I will start by saying that I thought I had kindness pretty figured out. But I realised that it is far more complex than I could have imagined. That everything links back to kindness, and success comes from understanding that.

This book has been seven years in the making and has taken several trips around the world meeting extraordinary people who demonstrate kindness throughout their everyday lives, podcast interviews with many guests (https://www.nahlasummers.com/podcast), and hundreds of conversations on kindness.

In this time I also founded Sunshine People. Sunshine People is where I and others complete adventurous challenges that are far beyond our capabilities. Rather than asking the world to give financial donations, instead we ask for support by doing an act of kindness for a stranger.

What I found is that, completely by accident, I was suddenly collecting stories of kindness. You know when everyone gives you something that they know you are interested in for a gift, well I was getting not only stories but people clambering to be kinder to me personally.

By starting a conversation about kindness, it had given permission for people to in turn do an act of kindness towards those around them and want to share the impact of that. Kindness, as I like to say, breeds kindness. However, my question was why did so many need that permission and reminder to be kinder?

I spent 15 years in the corporate world within leadership. A few years in each company gave me a full view of what has been happening in leadership for many years and why the UK is becoming less and less productive. Coupled with some serious reflection on my own weaknesses, I was able to use these experiences and this knowledge throughout the book.

Kindness is not easy and is not an easy conversation piece. We often choose not to accept kindness, and to talk about it is somehow uncouth to many. However, on the Sunshine People 2019 challenge of walking 500 miles from the south to the north of England, the strangest realisation happened. I had to rely on people to put me up, feed me and support the walk. I had asked my friends who had stepped up to support, however in the places I didn't have anywhere to stay I had to put out a post on social media to ask if anyone would help. The response was astonishing. The post was shared hundreds of times and I had so many messages I was unable to keep up. On this walk I quickly got over my difficulties of accepting kindness, having a conversation about it and sharing the impacts. I will talk more about that idea within this book and the effects on you and the wider world.

This book is intended for leaders, HR professionals and individuals looking to make a culture that they are happy to work within. It aims to give understanding to the different elements of how to achieve this and what benefits it can bring. From reading the book, completing the activities and, if you feel so inclined, then the online course, you will see that the success you receive from building this sort of culture is endless. It is not just one act of kindness, it is a way of life.

I hope to inspire some discussions within your workplace or establishment on how you can put this into practice. Do get in touch if you would like your business to take part in a program of change that measures the improvements to the wellbeing and retention of employees, and of profitability for the company, while embedding a culture of kindness within it.

Kindness, as I have come to experience it, is very much like happiness. It is contagious, we are simply three degrees of separation away from every act that we have given out. There is evidence that our happiness increases by 25 percent by being around someone happy. I have come to believe from my experience that the same is likely to also apply for kindness.

Kindness as I see it has come into fashion, or it may be a sign of the times. As we develop, so too does the need or simple desire to be kind. We will discuss when this tends to happen within the book. I suggest that this book should not be used in isolation, even though that would certainly help the reader grow as an individual. To get a greater benefit, the members of your team or organisation will need to adopt a culture of kindness and take the actions within the book together. This is the way you will see a global positive change. I hope you will enjoy the journey.

To You
I see you shine through in every act of kindness.
Love Me.

Acknowledgements

First, a thank you to Pinky Lilani, writer of the Foreword who I am very fortunate to have met and is the embodiment of how to make a culture of kindness. Through her work creating the Kindness in Leadership awards she gives us hope for a future that allows kindness to be at the forefront of all workplaces in the future.

Special thanks goes to all those that have featured in Season 1 of the podcast and of which some of those have also been quoted within the book. It is an incredible mix of wonderful humans ready to share their wisdom of how bringing kindness into life and leadership has been invaluable to their success.

Guillermo Donadini, Chief Investment Officer – General Insurance (Ex-Japan) at AIG.
Jackie Scully, Deputy Managing Director, Think.
Rebecca Robins, Global Chief Learning and Culture Officer, and Head of Global luxury practice, Interbrand.
Mrs Rachel Sayles BA Hons, Head of Humanities and PSHE, Hayesfield School.
Sally Waterston, Non-Executive Chair of Waterstons Ltd.
Emma Sergeant, President Europe, DAS Group of Companies (a division of Omnicom).
Simon Kempton, Operational Policing Lead for the Police Federation of England and Wales.
Pippa Richardson, Director, The Head Shed and Shed the Conflict.
Sean Tompkins, CEO RICS.
Byron Vincent, Writer, Performer, Broadcaster.
Valeria Locatelli, Audit Director, M&G Investments.
Phil Smith, Chairman at IQE, Prev. CEO of Cisco.
Emma Slade, Founder of Opening your Heart to Bhutan

Ricky Manetta, Founder of MMA Krav Maga and a head coordinator with the UFC.

Dani Saveker, Founder of the Glas Group, Visual Synopsis and Inspire kindness movement.

Dr Sanjav Nichani, Founder of Healing little Hearts.

Samantha-Jane Littlejohns, Therapist and Coach, creator of The Habits of Happiness and founder of Thee Happiness Hub.

Benjamin Mathes, Founder, Urban confessional.

Amber Dee, Artist/Songwriter.

Clayton Planter, Founder, Street 2 Boardroom.

Andy Sammons, Author of the Compassionate Teacher.

Josh Connolly, Life leadership and performance coach, Freedom From Within.

Pinky Lilani CBE DL, Chairman, Women of the Future Programme & Asian Women of Achievement Awards.

Becky Kroger, Points of Light award winner.

Lord Mark Price, Founder of Engaging works, Prev. CEO Waitrose.

Tom Levitt, Writer and Consultant, Sector 4 Focus.

PJ Ellis, Co-Owner - Lightbox Digital Co-Founder – LoveBrum.

Nigel Prideaux, Communications Director, Aviva.

Dave Durocher, Executive Director, The Other Side Academy.

Caroline Diehl MBE, Founder of the Social Founder Network, and Founder & Chair, Together TV.

Fi Munro PhD, Motivational speaker and author.

Andy Craven - Griffith - Radio presenter, writer and performer.

A special thank you to Social Change (Social change.co.uk) who allowed me to use their online piece by Emily Rose (Rosie) within the book, it's a wonderful insightful article.

I'd like to thank all the people I have met who have shared stories of kindness. Those who have supported Sunshine People challenges with some form of kindness. You are all wonderful and this book could not in so many ways ever have even existed without you.

Mostly, I must thank the wonderful Jasmin Naim who was the independent editor to this book. She excelled herself by making this book better and stronger. She was honest as she provided her guidance and wisdom and best of all; she was incredibly kind.

A Culture of Kindness

1. What is kindness?

Kindness is about a genuine authenticity, it's about something that flows through everything you do whether it's seen or unseen but particularly when it's unseen.

Nigel Prideaux, Communications Director, Aviva

1.1 Discussion on the history of kindness

There appears to be a circular pattern with kindness over the centuries. One that is fed through the culture at the time in that particular country.

It appears that only when we sink to the lowest places as a society through poor politics, death, natural disaster or such like does kindness have a chance to be more prevalent. Like the desperation for water in a drought.

Ask anyone who lived through the World Wars and they will tell you that people took care of their neighbours. They gave relief to their enemy in the quiet times of self reflection. It would seem unusual when our backs are up against the wall that we don't necessarily go into protection mode, but that something shines through us and allows us to be vulnerable. That ultimately the need for human connection is greater. I believe that at the heart of everything, as humans we recognise that we need each other to survive. To be the last man standing does not encourage our survival as a species.

A fundamental wave of kindness appears to have rolled through the ages of our development as society. However, there are several things that shock me. First, that some of the philosophers who preached kindness appeared not to be inherently and consistently kind within their own lives. One such man, Jean-Jacques Rousseau, 17th Century philosopher had given his children up to orphanages citing that his 'wife's family would have ruined them'. On the face of it we wonder, well why keep having children? Why not challenge yourself to change the fate that you are already predicting? However, was his kindness true in the fact the children's lives would have been better at an orphanage? You, the reader, and I probably find it hard to believe. However, there we have it. I have learnt that our stories are not the same, we cannot fully understand the motivations of another until we make steps to walk in their shoes. We must all take steps to consider the effects of our actions, to heighten our self-awareness, and the effects of those actions on our relationships.

When you look at the techniques the Stoics used to be happy, it is clear that they had already identified the power of emotional intelligence. However, with kindness they also understood that the very essence of being human is to help other humans.

Their four cardinal virtues were wisdom, justice, courage and temperance.

Wisdom (or moral wisdom as it is easier to understand)
This is based on the idea of your personal knowledge of good and bad or right and wrong. Also, it means understanding what is important in life and what you should allow to affect you. It is the ability and wisdom to give yourself wise counsel.

Justice
This focuses on morality as a whole and more importantly for this book, kindness. Marcus Aurelius wrote about this in particular in *The*

Meditations. It refers to the need to have goodwill towards individuals and society as a whole to truly have purpose.

A human being is formed by nature to benefit others, and, when he has performed some benevolent action or accomplished anything else that contributes to the common good, he has done what he was constituted for, and has what is properly his.

Marcus Aurelius, Meditations

Courage

As we understand it in this era, courage allows us to endure pain, to endure fear and do it anyway. The discipline of fear and the desire to control it if you like.

Temperance

This is based on the ideas of being in control and having awareness of self. Stoics' beliefs were something like mindfulness, although my research suggests it is better defined as an ancient idea of emotional intelligence and, more specifically, self-management.

The Roman statesman Cicero, not a Stoic as previously discussed, stated that it was more natural to feel kindness towards family than anyone else. But he also stated that people who cared more for their fellow citizens than for foreigners threatened to tear apart the fellowship that unites mankind. It's a theory that we see today in politics which prioritises kindness that is given to the few and not to the many. This somehow implies that they believe that human kindness can run out, and that if we include all the people in our acts of kindness this will somehow endanger ourselves and our nearest and dearest.

Freud talked about kindness in some unusual ways, namely in a sexual context. He also believed, however, that aggression can also constitute kindness. That when aggression happens that it is simply a wish for more intimate exchange.

Of course, no book on kindness can choose to omit the parable of the good Samaritan. Christianity was one of the catalysts for kindness being generalised to how and when to carry out kind acts within our communities. Kindness was not only seen as a way to live well through this 'good Samaritan' approach but it also became a moral law similar to the Stoic ideals. Morals are simply actions that we decide as a person or community to be essentially good or bad. 'To love thy neighbour as thyself'. But, 'who is my neighbour?' is the question. For those unfamiliar with the parable of the good Samaritan, it describes an Israelite who had been robbed and injured and left by the roadside. Everyone passed by without giving help, including Israelites. However, it was the Samaritan who stopped and helped, even though they were known to be enemy of the Israelites. Hence, the 'Good Samaritan'.

It's interesting to imagine if every person before us had avoided following in the footsteps of this good Samaritan, and instead had always chosen to be the person that passed by the injured Israelite; where might the world be now and would we exist at all? There are many views on whether kindness and the actions of the 'good Samaritan' are in fact built within us or, for those who are religious, if it is God who allows us to be kind.

The book *Leviathan* was published in 1668 and it is considered the earliest written social contract theory. The author, Thomas Hobbes, appears to have believed that good and evil are the prevailing facets of the human condition within politics. This is a topic that, at the time of writing, has become a topic of despair for many. 'The state of nature' is the term Hobbes used for the concept of the way of life before society was developed.

Mozi was the first philosopher believed to develop this idea. He thought that each person has their own rule, and each a differing moral compass. In other words, that there are no general rules for society, and because of this simple social order not being met, food would be wasted, and secrecy over wisdom would be commonplace. This means that society could not grow without order. Some would argue that this applies equally with social order in modern times. That now greed leads to food wastage on a global level, and that wisdom is kept for the few and not for the greater good, leading the divide between rich and poor to grow ever larger with time.

Hobbes believed that, without a societal law, each person would be against every other person. He uses the term, 'War of all against all'. It meant that nothing could be owned, that there would be no legal system and no common rights. We are a long way from that in western cultures, and our current society has changed and adapted, but many of our societal structures have remained the same as when they were first formed, such as our political system for example. This gives rise to some basic concerns about how our social contracts need to change. Kindness is not a social contract, it is an unwritten moral law. One, that if not followed, has no consequences. When I spoke with CEOs about this, they mentioned the idea of making kindness a performance criterion, to make sure that unkindness is not tolerated and would be ousted from our communities and workplaces. Social contracts are therefore whatever we decide them to be in our culture.

There is a man currently depicted on the English £20 note and in small letters under his image is the name, Adam Smith. By 2020 he will have been replaced by a new design, which I believe is ironic. Adam Smith is better known for authoring the 'The Wealth of Nations', in which he outlines what we now call behavioural economics a couple of centuries before it even existed. However, his mind while great focused not just on one thing, he saw the big picture. In his earlier work, *The Theory of Moral Sentiments*, he discusses what motivates people to behave in the ways they do. Much of his wisdom on success, good morals and of course kindness, or as he termed it, 'benevolence', still resonates today. This is evident in his opening sentence,

How selfish soever man may be supposed, there are evidently some principles in his nature, which interest him in the fortune of others, and render their happiness necessary to him, though he derives nothing from it except the pleasure of seeing it.

Smith advises that humans are inherently selfish but that equally we naturally will walk in a fellow human's shoes in times of their distress and watch over them then. Ultimately we feel what they might be feeling. However, he goes on to state that we will also become intolerant of each other when this empathy wanes and for all humans the need and concern back to self will always prevail.

Philosophy of kindness brings up lots of varying opinions. Paul Kjellberg talks of an interesting concept of the link between kindness and learning through the Chinese teaching of Confucianism in a section of his blog post titled 'Intelligent kindness':

Usually when we think of an education, we think of it as the accumulation of information. While information plays an important role, a Confucian education is more a process of self-cultivation. Specifically, it is a process of becoming intelligently kind.

Like liberal education, Confucian education is not directed toward any particular form of employment. But as with a liberal education, one could use almost any form of employment to act kindly. Though he also sees kindness as an end in itself, Confucius also thinks that people who approach the task this way will ultimately be the most effective.
What does it mean to be "intelligently kind"? People can be kind without being intelligent and intelligent without being kind. Success for Confucius was learning to be both at the same time. Obviously by

"kindness" here we mean something more than just being nice all the time since sometimes you have to be if not cruel to be kind, at least sanguine.

We tend to think of kindness as a feeling or a passion. Etymologically, a passion is something that happens to you, as opposed to an action, which is something you do. But Confucius, along with Aristotle and others in the West, think of at least some feelings as things we can cultivate, practice, and strengthen. (1)

There is something interesting in this Confucian way. It preaches respect for elders, and for one another, advocating treating others in a way that you would want them to treat you. The ideals centre around humanism and perfecting the human being, based on morals that have become rules to live by. Adherents all understand the teaching and seek to live more harmoniously because of it.

However, Kjellberg is saying here that we tend to think of kindness as a feeling or a passion. For the purposes of this book and in my work, kindness is the action that provokes a feeling or passion. The ancient mindset that we can cultivate, practice and strengthen our feelings I believe to be correct. We do that by our actions and this in its simplest term is *emotional intelligence.*

The simple phenomenon of kindness has in the past got me thinking about how it has been around for so many years but yet is discussed so infrequently. Our differences, as we grow as a society, get larger. Between our increasing variety of religions, generations, cultures, opinions, traditions, and upbringings it means our interpretation of the things that bind us are not always universal. However kindness, like a smile, appears to be a consistent message throughout history. An act of kindness can be delivered as an action and, while the emotion it provokes can be very different, the message is always the same. 'I see you, I am here, I care.'

Ian Maclaren (rev Dr John Watson) who was a minister for the Free Church of Scotland in the early 19th Century is credited with the famous line, 'Be kind, for everyone you meet is fighting a hard battle.' (Or if you would like to believe others, it was in fact Plato or Philo of Alexandria who coined this phrase.)

Whichever era this quote came from, I think we can agree that some things in the human realm never change. Times for those who lean towards the pessimistic view of life have never been tougher than they have right now. The usual reaction in tough times may be to withdraw from others because they are so consumed by their own internal story. This is the battle that Ian Maclaren talks about. However, when we do withdraw, that's when in fact a sense of loneliness and isolation will make that battle a little tougher.

As I know from experience, a simple act of kindness can reconnect someone who has decided to go into their own head back to the world. Ten brief minutes have the power to change lives. Irrespective of how simple the act you are extending to another person may seem, universally speaking, there's no such thing as a small act of kindness. Every act of kindness creates a ripple effect which reaches out far beyond your act. That's the empowering thing about kindness, when we receive kindness we are naturally inspired to extend it to others.

This leads me to share with you the power of the ten minutes that changed my life in the midst of my partner's death.

It had been a stranger who had approached me on a rare moment of leaving the house about six weeks or so after his death. That stranger told me a story that was of positivity. He didn't ask me about my story or why I had looked so sad, but by sparing me ten minutes of his time, unconsciously said, 'I see you, I am here, I care.' It was the catalyst for me starting in those first days to function again and then eventually to start to climb literal mountains. As Maclaren says, we do know the battle, but

A Culture of Kindness

history shows us we don't necessarily need to understand it fully to make a change.

Coming back to religion, each one has love and kindness at the heart of its message. Christianity, as discussed, speaks of the good Samaritan and the need to love your neighbour. In Hinduism, Gandhi speaks of the religion that holds dear 'the virtue of compassion to all living beings', and when I interviewed Emma Slade, financier turned Buddhist, she tells of the seed that is within us all and grows with kindness. The Dalai Lama highlights that compassion is not a luxury, but a question of human survival. *The greatest degree of inner tranquility comes from the cultivation of love and compassion. The more we care for the happiness of others, the greater is our own sense of well-being.*
Kindness goes hand in hand with compassion. I believe compassion is the feeling within every act of kindness, and while the two are not the same, they are very similar. Compassion is the core value shared by many religions, which is interesting as often the other ideals can so differ.

Although we are individuals, throughout history religion has aimed to bring people together for the greater good. While others may have attempted to exploit that along the way, the truth is we are intrinsically linked and the greatest things in history have happened through a coming together of humans with love and kindness. The Dalai Lama writes, *This is my simple religion. There is no need for temples; no need for complicated philosophy. Our own brain, our own heart is our temple; the philosophy is kindness.*

1.2 Preconceived ideas

Kindness unlocks something for businesses that has never been more important and relevant.

Jackie Scully, Deputy Managing Director, Think

Many ideas in this world are already labelled and those labels are firmly fixed; it's just what we collectively do as human beings. We like to label and box things and we do it to everything: people, products, you name it. Kindness is no exception. Kindness is generally not a word that is to be used beyond primary school. In the corporate world it is seen by many as fluffy and not in line with the values of any company that aims at performing highly, or certainly not for inclusion in their mission statement.

This book weighs this up and identifies the need to actively seek out kindness within organisations using the steps I have laid out. I interviewed hundreds of people and will continue to do so far beyond this book, delving into the reasons for what makes them believe acts of kindness are more important than any other in terms of leading to success.

When I asked people what a culture of kindness meant to them, their answers were wide and varied which was not something I expected. However, a familiar theme running through those answers was the question, 'Isn't that what we are all working towards?'

All over the world and even in New Zealand where they had a really terrible tragedy, the Prime Minister said it is kindness that will repair the world. Such a huge crisis, and what did she go back to, the most basic human values, kindness.

Pinky Lilani CBE, DL

Imagine how productive the world would become! So, where does this come from if we know that we are all flawed, selfish and need to be kinder to each other? Why do we continue to be unkind and not address this? Several things came to light in my studies of kindness and the next chapter deals with a major contributor, fear. As I see it, several other factors are involved, as elaborated below.

First is people's reluctance to discuss their own acts of kindness. It is somehow seen as uncouth to share such stories, as though we are telling the world we are greater than we are because we dare to share. It is seen by some to be showing off, and generally something not to be discussed. However, society learns through stories, and this has been the case since the beginning of time. The more stories we share of kindness, human connection and goodness then the more seeds we plant into the ears of the listeners that in time grow into new habits.

Secondly, there is the idea that to be kind is to show a level of weakness. In fact, it's not simply weakness, but the ability to be vulnerable which actually demonstrates great strength. In many respects we have to allow ourselves to be vulnerable to in turn be truly kind. To approach someone to ask if they might need a hand with something, or to talk with the stranger on the street because they look sad for example, brings all our vulnerabilities to the surface.

Thirdly, saying no is considered unkind. There are families in which some parents can't say no to their children, perhaps believing it is some form of unkindness to do that. The age-old proverb springs to mind, 'You have to be cruel to be kind'. The issue is that the boundaries of cruelty have always been open to interpretation and so this has become an unpopular phrase. However if your child each day after school asks for sweets, and you never say no because you don't want to be unkind in that immediate moment, in the long term you are actually being unkind, not only in relation to their health but also their understanding of boundaries. The same goes for not being honest about behaviours that are not socially popular, appeasing a person to 'keep the peace' in the long term does not help them grow and develop healthy relationships with others.

Fourthly, there is the word kindness itself. We can ask a person in a position of power to have compassion or empathy which has a lesser connotation of letting our guard down or being too 'fluffy'. Kindness, however, lies in the acts we deliver that demonstrate we have compassion and empathy and therefore kindness is at the heart of our very being. It is of course about one act but it is also about exhibiting kindness in all of your actions and this comes down to adopting a set of qualities in your everyday life. These and how to deliver them are set out in Chapter 4.2.

Historically kindness is seen as a feminine trait and even in those languages which specify gender it tends to take the feminine. In a world which in many cases is attempting to be more accepting of others, it is unsurprising that male senior leaders are being encouraged to adopt a leadership approach which embraces kindness to see the best in their people.

My favourite translation of kindness is the Estonian which translates as 'Head-us'. It feels to me a coming together of our minds, that somehow we are all affected by each other's kindness through our mental health. Which is in fact now becoming scientifically proven, but more on that later.

Selfishness is something within all of us, it is a trait and with that many believe kindness to be a luxury. Something to be given on special occasions only. Psychologists might say that kindness does not come naturally. On one hand I would agree, as we all fight with the inner demons that our minds pull us back to. Although I am curious as I am not so sure Mother Teresa had this issue, Sadhi or any other advocate of kindness. In the book *On Kindness* they say, *At its strongest we have to believe that feeling too much for others – being too sympathetic – either endangers our lives or is against our natures.* Which takes us smoothly into the fear of kindness.

1.3 Fear of kindness

Where are we with kindness as a whole? I think it is essential, if we do not have kindness towards ourselves, others and our planet, we won't have a planet. It's grown so fast that if we do not work together with compassion and kindness we will no longer be here. We cannot survive in a selfish bubble because it's all simply led by fear.

Samantha-Jane, Happiness Coach and Founder of the
Thee Happiness Hub

The fear of kindness dawned on me quite early in my interest in this topic so I would like to share with you a couple of personal stories that piqued this interest. I often talk about this 'fear of kindness' that appears to lie within us all as so many of the conversations lead back to it. It has become pivotal in my search for how we find a way back to each other.

Sometime late in 2013 when the weather was not too cool for the time of year, I drove past a single middle-aged lady looking to catch a lift, standing on a slip road that led onto the motorway. I had hesitated a little too long to be able to pull over and ended up on the motorway. It bugged me so much that I drove all the way to the next junction before turning around and heading back again, which was a 20-mile round trip. She wasn't there when I got back, but I often think of it. Something small haunts me with the, 'I should have'.

Then about a year later as a vendor at a car boot sale, on driving into the queue to exit the field, I saw a lady carrying some heavy bags. I thought she must have a car near, but in my rear-view mirror I watched her walk up the hill, clearly not reaching a car. I think about that moment often as she struggled some 300 metres to the top of the field. Why didn't I stop and just ask rather than regretfully looking in my rear-view mirror? I think about these as examples of where my fear overtook my decision not to stop.

I say fear in its loosest sense. Our brains take a moment to evaluate a situation and, in those moments when we question whether to go and lend a hand to someone, we think of all the possible outcomes. 'Oh, they will be ok', 'what if they say 'no thanks'', 'what if they are insulted by the offer', 'what if they reject my offer', or 'they could take advantage of my kindness'.

In reality, the worst possible answers to the above questions really have little impact on us if we don't allow them to. Rejection, hurt ego, fear of any danger we could put ourselves in. We stop ourselves from doing so much in those vital first moments when we think of helping because we overthink and allow fear to take over.

Some people don't possess this fear, there aren't many of them but they do exist. My partner was one of them, he once picked up a young girl who was clearly drunk on a cold dark road, but had she continued she would have died from the cold or been picked up by someone not as kind, he actually did have reason to have fear for there were a number of things that he could have been accused of, but he dropped her off where she wanted to go, made sure she was safe, and called the police to explain the situation and where he had dropped her. He didn't hesitate, he just knew that was what he had to do. He was the sort of person who would wait for the lift doors to shut and then start up polite conversation with the strangers riding the lift with him. At first I used to cringe, but you soon change because when you experience someone's kindness given without fear it becomes so infectious. You realise in fact there is nothing to fear.

After a recent talk I gave a father asked me during the Q&A section how to encourage our children to be kind but also keep them safe? I have given this question considerable thought since he asked it. In essence the answer is all about fear and judgement. The fear we feel about protecting our young is as old as human existence, however the media and the stories that are written to generate shock and fear are not. The stories of death, destruction and abductions are produced in such a way we can start to believe that our neighbour could well be the next Jack the Ripper. Fear is fed to us as adults and we pass that fear onto our children even as we teach them to read and write. We don't trust first, we fear first.

Fear is built into our brains to help us sense danger that could ultimately maim or kill us. It used to be sabre-tooth tigers we were fighting. Now in the modern day we have so much more to make us fearful. Our media and social media mean that we are often exposed to stories that show us the worst of human beings. People become fearful of a group that has been labelled dangerous because one person within that group has done something outside of societal laws.

Byron Vincent, writer, performer and broadcaster, when asked about the connection between this and mental health said the following, *Sabre tooth tigers? Our brains haven't evolved much in the last ten thousand years. Our threat responses are great at dealing with sabre-tooth tigers, fight it, hide from it or run away from it. Simple. They're not so great at dealing with the constant barrage of complex anxieties the modern world throws our way. To our brains all threats are potential sabre tooth tigers. Our Twitter feed is full of tigers, our Facebook feed is full of tigers, Newspaper headlines are Tigers. Fake news, Tigers. Advertising, Tigers. Every social interaction we have is ambush of tigers. It's relentless. Unfortunately, we live in a culture that exploits our anxiety to sell us stuff so the mechanism that once protected us from being eaten by predators, ends up being an endless trigger for unnecessary spikes in our anxiety. This is why more than ever we must be mindful about where we choose to feed our brains. Everything we take in will inform our future behaviour and reactions.*

The anxiety and fear is triggered in the brain in very much the same way. We must consider that it is what we willingly feed our brains that in turn causes our behaviours and reactions.

But what Professor Dacher Keltner, Director of the Berkeley Social Interaction Laboratory, says is that in fact we are wired for goodness. In his interview with David DiSalvo, he shares that his Darwin-inspired studies have revealed that our capacity for caring, for play, for reverence and modesty are built into our brains, bodies, genes and social practices. He states that, while most believe Darwin was focused on proving we were aggressive and competitive, his research showed that Darwin actually believed human caring was inbuilt. He gives us these two important takeaways from his research: (2)

The first takeaway is found in the Descent of Man, where Darwin argues that we are a profoundly social and caring species. This idea is reflected in the two quotes below, where Darwin argues that our tendencies toward sympathy are instinctual and evolved (and not some cultural construct as so many have assumed), and even stronger (or perhaps more ethical—see his observation about the "timid man" below) than the instinct for self-preservation:

For firstly, the social instincts lead an animal to take pleasure in the society of his fellows, to feel a certain amount of sympathy with them, and to perform various services for them. … Such actions as the above appear to be the simple result of the greater strength of the social or maternal instincts than that of any other instinct or motive; for they are performed too instantaneously for reflection, or for pleasure or even misery might be felt. In a timid man, on the other hand, the instinct of self-preservation might be so strong, that he would be unable to force himself to run any such risk, perhaps not even for his own child."

The second take away comes from close study of Darwin's 'Expression of Emotion in Man and Animals', published one year after the 'Descent of Man'. There, Darwin details descriptions of emotions such as reverence, love, tenderness, laughter, embarrassment and the conceptual tools to document the evolutionary origins of these emotions. That led me to my own work on the physiology and display of these remarkable emotions, and to the science-based conclusion that these emotions lie at the core of our capacities for virtue and cooperation.

There is so much contradiction in how we perceive our greatest minds as well as our attitudes towards religion. Both society and animal instincts have moved on so much. Although we still have largely the same brain function, and release the same hormones, the expression of those fears has changed considerably. We are in a more emotive society.

What has been very interesting in this journey is that emotions are what drive us to be kind to each other. How we manage those emotions is key to how we interact with each other and will become the basis for Chapter 5a5.

A Culture of Kindness

1.4   Side-effects of kindness

I am going to introduce the idea of Telomeres. This stems from one of the most interesting pieces of research about how our behaviours and habits affect our health.

Dr. Elizabeth Blackburn is a molecular biologist who in 2009 won the Nobel Prize for Medicine for her discovery of telomeres and the key enzyme associated with their functioning (telomerase). With Dr. Elissa Epel, an accomplished health psychologist, whose research has focused on stress, ageing and obesity, she wrote *The Telomere Effect* (3). Together they are a powerhouse of science and practical, clear and feasible wisdom that applies to us all. So, let me elaborate...

Blackburn states, *If you think of your chromosomes – which carry your genetic material – as shoelaces, telomeres are the little protective tips at the end. They are made of repeating short sequences of DNA sheathed in special proteins.*
During our lives they tend to wear down and when telomeres can't protect chromosomes properly, cells can't replenish and they malfunction. This sets up physiological changes in the body which increase risks of the major conditions and diseases of ageing: cardiovascular disease, diabetes, cancer, a weakened immune system and more. But the process is somewhat malleable. It is happening in all of us at some rate, but the rate can change. An enzyme called telomerase can add DNA to the ends of chromosomes to slow, prevent and partially reverse the shortening.

So the idea is that you want to elongate your telomeres to avoid poor health and extend your life. Telomeres can change in length, in quite short periods of time with the wrong habits. Telomerase is what is added to prevent the shortening.

The study highlights and quantifies the mind-body connection in scientific terms, proving that meditation, mindfulness, yoga, Qigong and similar do in fact lengthen life. We are what we eat, so eating more Omega 3, staying off processed foods, white bread, sugary drinks, all the things we already know are bad for us, actually do shorten our telomeres. Exercise is very important, but not in hardcore and extreme forms, consistent and gentle is fine. It is clear that mixing up different exercise regimes, appears to enhance the length of telomeres.

The relevant point here is the impact of behaviour on our health. Being around people that you can trust and forming healthy human connections have the power to keep telomeres long, hence the impact of kindness.

Conscientiousness is also believed to be a personality trait that encourages healthy telomeres and therefore long life. So many of the things covered in this book will help to increase your conscientiousness. Good news!

I cannot talk about the effects of kindness without touching on David Hamilton's work including many books on the subject. His website features a great article that summarises his work, although the book is recommended also. He writes: (4)

Kindness makes us happier

On a biochemical level, it is believed that the good feeling we get is due to elevated levels of the brain's natural versions of morphine and heroin, which we know as endogenous opioids. They cause elevated levels of dopamine in the brain and so we get a natural high, often referred to as 'Helper's High'.

Kindness is good for the heart

A Culture of Kindness

Acts of kindness are often accompanied by emotional warmth. Emotional warmth produces the hormone, oxytocin, in the brain and throughout the body. Of recent interest is its significant role in the cardiovascular system.

Oxytocin causes the release of a chemical called nitric oxide in blood vessels, which dilates (expands) the blood vessels. This reduces blood pressure and therefore oxytocin is known as a 'cardioprotective' hormone because it protects the heart (by lowering blood pressure). The key is that acts [of] kindness can produce oxytocin and therefore kindness can be said to be cardioprotective.

Kindness slows ageing

But remarkable research now shows that oxytocin (that we produce through emotional warmth) reduces levels of free radicals and inflammation in the cardiovascular system and so slows ageing at source. Incidentally these two culprits also play a major role in heart disease so this is also another reason why kindness is good for the heart.

There have also been suggestions in the scientific journals of the strong link between compassion and the activity of the vagus nerve. The vagus nerve, as well as regulating heart rate, also controls inflammation levels in the body.

Kindness improves relationships

We are wired for kindness.
Our evolutionary ancestors had to learn to cooperate with one another. The stronger the emotional bonds within groups, the greater were the chances of survival and so 'kindness genes' were etched into the human genome.

So today when we are kind to each other we feel a connection and new relationships are forged, or existing ones strengthened.

Kindness is contagious

When we're kind we inspire others to be kind and studies show that it actually creates a ripple effect that spreads outwards to our friends' friends' friends – to 3-degrees of separation. Just as a pebble creates waves when it is dropped in a pond, so acts of kindness ripple outwards touching others' lives and inspiring kindness everywhere the wave goes.

It starts to become clear even from a basic human level that kindness makes sense. However, from a business point of view it goes even deeper and has the power to change business as we know it.

A Culture of Kindness

2. What is unkindness?

I have learned silence from the talkative, toleration from the intolerant, and kindness from the unkind.

Khalil Gibran

Unkindness
noun

noun: **unkindness**; plural noun: **unkindnesses**
Inconsiderate and harsh behaviour
'she had had enough of her father's unkindness'
synonyms: nastiness, unpleasantness, disagreeableness, cruelty, spite, malice, meanness, mean-spiritedness, viciousness, malevolence, uncharitableness and so on.
Antonyms: Kindness
(Oxford Dictionary)

Interestingly, use of the word unkindness in literature (according to Google word search) has declined in the past 200 years. However, 'meanness' seems to have increased. The words that we use take on a different slant depending on how we see the severity of a situation. Kindness and unkindness have equally declined in use. In contrast, usage of the word compassion is steadily increasing over the past 50 years. The word empathy was really uncommon up until the 1950s when it became popular. The use of words is hugely important and I believe is often underrated. As an NLP master practitioner I understand the power a single word can have. This relevance and importance applies equally to an individual but also a group setting for leadership.

Maybe you've been part of a group setting when someone has been upset by something, and another person has asked, 'Can't you take a joke'. There might be a few others who may not have laughed either and the moment is hurried on and quickly forgotten, or an attempt is made to anyway. The issue here is these things are rarely taken out of context for the individual.

Kindness as a word is out of favour. However, we must focus on the actions of kindness and unkindness if we are to succeed.

2.1 Examples of unkindness

I feel it is a high-pressured environment, (Finance sector) it is a competitive environment. There is a lot of dog-eat-dog because people are competing for bonuses and they are competing with each other most of the time. So, everyone wants to be the smartest one in the room. That's the nature of that world. So there is a lot of repression of humanity, it is difficult to admit weakness, to admit you are having a hard time and it's a work-driven culture, a culture that doesn't want to know if you have children or you have ageing parents or you are struggling with schooling. That is the nature of it. It is a difficult environment with its own form of suffering. Intellectually it's very stimulating but for the whole human being I think it's a challenging environment but I believe that has been recognised and institutions are rethinking how they address wellbeing and look after the staff.

Emma Slade, Founder of 'Opening your heart to Bhutan'

Unkindness is a topic as big as kindness. However here I want to share with you some stories of unkindness and highlight the little things that don't seem very obvious.

Rachel Roberts writes in The Independent a story in 1996 of her experience on a Number 4 bus going from Islington to Tufnell Park in London. (5) Be warned you will be saddened. She describes the moment that an old woman who was beside her had a heart attack and fell face down on the bus steps.

She went to help but to her horror realised that no one else on the bus was coming to help her. The bus was still moving and getting the lady into a recovery position was becoming a challenge. Everyone else on the bus either stared out the window or at them as they struggled to help the woman. In the end, it was she that had to shout at the bus driver to stop.

As they waited for an ambulance, a few people got off, stepping over the lady as they passed with no acknowledgment.

She recalls the moment that the ambulance arrived and that moment when suddenly this 'paralysis' of the other passengers had disappeared and people were 'tripping over themselves' to tell them what had happened and the stories were varied. She describes it as turning into a circus. Deciding it was better to walk away, she then left it to the professionals. At the end of her article she asks, *'Is this the price you pay for living in London? People simply don't care, too wrapped up in their lives to bother about one another. I do not blame people for not getting involved in every situation. It can be dangerous.*

But that day, there were no excuses. She was a helpless old lady who suffered the humiliation of having a heart attack in public.'

Roberts is right, in my opinion, there are no excuses, however I am interested as to why. At that time the UK was just coming out of a recession. We know for sure the things that go on in a country affect the way people treat each other. If we look at the 2012 Olympics in the UK, the mood of the nation was upbeat and forward thinking. We were brought together by a common desire to succeed. The Olympics started to unite a nation that had lost its lustre. Sports personalities defied the odds, spending years working towards being victorious. We sat and willed them on through our TVs, growing stronger with every medal that was won. I wonder if that same lady had had a heart attack in 2012 with those same people on the bus, if in fact they would have checked on her, stepped up to the plate and shown the empathy that Roberts had expected from fellow human beings.

We are so affected by our environment but humans very rarely let that account for our behaviours or reactions. It is so true even of our daily working environments. We are motivated or not by what we see, smell, hear, as well as relative comfort and lighting. If we have the news circling in the background with its sadness and tragedy, that impacts our motivation. If we work in a place that has comfortable seating and natural light, that impacts our motivation. Our environments are not just made up of our immediate influences, but also those factors that affect our village, town, country and the world as a whole.

There is also the interesting point within Rachel Roberts' story about it being in London. She believed that the city had something to do with the reactions of her fellow bus riders, and initially I would have agreed with her. Many years ago, I was in Bangkok gaining my coaching qualification. I was at lunch with others from the course and we were talking about kindness (I do talk about other things). A lady mentioned that she ventured from the city to the countryside for the first time ever just the year before. She had been overwhelmed by the kindness of those in the countryside and had been given fruit which she had thought was a rare and unusual act of kindness. It had stuck with her as people rarely spoke to each other in the city. She didn't know who her neighbours were and the sense of community appeared absent.

What I have seen is a pattern that allows people in the city to be more closed. This has been backed by a recent UK study that shows that 'People in rural areas are more likely than those in towns or cities to experience kindness'. (6) This could be for a number of reasons, such as elevated crime rates which make us fear smiling at strangers and bringing danger to ourselves. Helping a stranger could result in dealing with someone with a whole host of issues you feel ill-equipped to deal with. Many people who have drug or alcohol addiction, are homeless or have severe mental health issues can get lost in a city and seek out some comfort from being with people.

In her story Roberts highlights that the people on the bus looked up only when the paramedics got there, then they all had something to say. She found this frustrating but I see why it happened. We are fearful creatures. Fear exists to protect us from dangerous situations. While Roberts dealt with the situation without fear, others could not. That was until a trained person, someone that felt like a figure of authority was present and they could then step forwards. Fear of doing the wrong thing, fear of making the situation worse is usually just a sign of a lack of confidence, but ultimately not stepping up reflects fear of so many things. They will feel shame of course, but at the time fear is stronger than the feeling of shame. Shame is the after-thought.

Looking at Charles Dickens' *A Christmas Carol,* Scrooge was a mean old man overtaken by greed and cruelty, his character is the epitome of unkindness. The ghosts of Christmas past and future visit and show him what could and would be. In the end as we know, kindness wins. An unwavering and continuous stream of standing strong, even in the face of the easy option, which is often unkindness. Eventually he submits to it. However, does this relate to real kindness or is it just a fairy tale?

As tough as it is, the evidence does seem to point towards the ability to drown out unkindness with a flowing river of kindness. We certainly know that unkindness does not stop if we are unkind in return. We simply start a battle of wills.

There is an interesting exercise that I do with young people and have seen others do too. You allow a person to be really unkind to you with their words and in return you are only accepting, nice and calm. Eventually they get stuck, they run out of words and in turn calm down. If you return those unkind words with further unkind words, it simply rages like oxygen fueling fire. It has to be stopped before you take the house down.

2.2 Consequences of unkindness

Emma Sergeant, President Europe, DAS Group of Companies, (a division of Omnicom), within the podcast interview I conducted with her provides a view on how to gain a kinder approach to leadership.

In a leadership role, we have to be intolerant of unkindness, when we see it, we must call it out. Bullying is the extreme and actually its simply unkindness that needs to be called out. To call it out will give us a culture of kindness.

You would think that unkindness is easily understood if it were simply the opposite of kindness, as kindness appears to be so easily understood. However, I have learnt that understanding unkindness on a human level goes much deeper. What one person can find unkind another has no problem with. We are all so different, unkindness and our perceptions of it also differ greatly.

The most obvious is the discarding of feelings. How often have you done this or witnessed it? It is most prevalent within the workplace. It is not seen as professional to share feelings in meetings, but only provide action and solutions, anything else would have people looking in their laps or checking their nails.

Let's say something is bothering you. You feel left out of a project or some work. You have a feeling of unease about something and you finally feel it is time to confront that situation. Someone is not telling you something and you feel that you are not in the loop. When you eventually tell your boss about your unease, they answer, 'What makes you think that?', not giving reassurance first before asking. Their flat tone is itself an instant answer. The boss has not been unkind in asking the question, but the unkindness has come from the lack of confirmation or denial. If they had confirmed that something was indeed going on in the background and they were sorry that you had felt that way, it would have not been unkind.

Why? Because honesty is never unkind when delivered with compassion. To leave someone not knowing, or feeling uneasy is unkindness. Sadly there are a considerable number of managers who do not deliver their messages with compassion.

Unless leaders make changes to how they react to employees' concerns, they will have an employee turnover that is costly to the company environment in more ways than one.

So, we might assume that the commonality in all humans is that we seek peace of mind. That we do not thrive off stress and that we are looking to remove that from our lives. Any perception of disconnect which we will term for now as unkindness, will not lead to overall wellbeing. When we adopt that understanding of unkindness and only tolerate transparency and honesty, striking out anything else, we start to build a culture of kindness.

So, what can being unkind entail?

Not listening to a person – when a person is truly heard it is indeed one of the kindest things you can offer. Not listening makes people feel disconnected and unheard.

'Not my problem' approach – an attempt to remove ourselves from a given situation. However, often that is the time that we really need to be stepping up and considering our future actions.

Promotion of stress – This started with the age of the 'work hard, play hard' ethos. How many times have you felt that you are in competition with someone over the hours you have worked? Maybe you feel compelled to explain the hours you have dedicated to something? We wear this work ethic as a badge of honour while barely sleeping and sinking into a quagmire of justifications. Those justifications are often because we feel unworthy or lack confidence, and consequently we need to be seen to overwork. We can't set boundaries and expectations to others. When you work through this book, I hope that you will feel better equipped to tackle that.

Sean Tompkins, Global CEO of RICS, believes that unkindness is linked intrinsically to distrust which he believes is rising. In fact, the statistics, which I will discuss later in this book, confirm that our trust in politicians is currently low, so let's touch on that for a moment. When discussing politics I acknowledge that I do this with some degree of bias. Having watched from the sidelines, and prior to starting to write this book, I knew very little of why the UK system involves people standing either side of a room shouting at each other.

This is democracy, so I am told. This is what we ask for; so that when we speak we are listened to. However, all this was set up before the world was at our fingertips as it is now. Obviously, there were many factors at play, but the essence of today's political scene is derived from the setting up of the Model Parliament of 1295. It was the dividing of two groups of people, nobility and higher clergy on one side, knights and burgesses on the other. No law of tax could pass effectively without them agreeing.

So, there are a couple of things that we need to consider as we look at the political system today. First, this system was formed 750 years ago. I think we can all admit that, by the time I have written even this sentence, technology will have already taken a giant step forwards somewhere in the world. 750 years ago, well we had never put a man on the moon, the idea seemed preposterous. They didn't have television or cinema. Not even a radio. Central heating, indoor plumbing were luxuries. The UK has gone from a population of 4 million to 56 million in that time. Times have changed and they will continue to change, it is simply the natural order of things. However, we still base our perceptions on a political system set up during feudal times. Some say the rich do still rule, but the populace at least now has a chance to have their say.

Of course, those knights that were first appointed to open parliament may well have had the people of their shire at the heart of what they wanted to deliver. However, that could not have applied to all of them. Certain psychological theories teach that we are all selfish. We are asked to believe that we have to try to suppress our innate selfishness and all other bad traits. That kindness is not the trait that first comes to us as a human being.

If that is the case, when we ask those people to stand up in parliament to speak for us, how can we truly expect them to speak for us, the poorer and lowlier in status? Surely, over the intervening 750 years, for some politicians, ego and power must have taken over, and they have prioritised their need for personal security and advantage?

Adding to this in this century, modern technology has allowed for quick statements to be made by keyboard warriors, and so politics is played out in a larger arena among the many. Arguments for and against certain current world developments come so thick and fast, with or without fact, it is too difficult to research which is valid or not. I asked Simon Kempton, Operational Policing Lead with the Police Federation of England and Wales (PFEW), about what his thoughts were about how we speak to each other about people through social media and he highlighted a very good point.

The rise in a populous politics opened the door for some behaviours that would have remained hidden, to now be exposed. People feel emboldened to be unpleasant in their opinions to others. Austerity had only just started then, but has ripped out the heart of public services, we have an excuse to use it to blame others. We saw this severe economic downturn and when that happens it opens the doors to these extreme views. Therefore, it's important through this to keep kindness at the forefront now more than ever. It will come around full circle but, in the meantime, it makes kindness even more important.

A Culture of Kindness

Kempton also mentioned the 2012 British Olympics and the impact he saw it have on the nation. The nation became a community and it brought the people together in a united front. We are divided so often and easily by the external factors being decided for us in the world. For many, to be unkind is an easier default position than to be kind. Kindness is something you have to dig deep for, to be a person who will allow people in, to be vulnerable and to know what love is.

3. Culture and kindness

It's roughly 2,000 years since some bloke got nailed to a tree for suggesting that we should all be a little bit nicer to each other and I fear over the last 2,000 years we haven't moved on very far from that. ... It really is something to do with treating people how we would want to be treated.

Simon Kempton, Operational Policing Lead, PFEW

Simon Kempton is quick to highlight that kindness is not a religious thing, that in fact this is a cultural thing. From what I have seen I would agree, every religion if you look at the heart of it, is all about kindness to others. The issue comes when this is interpreted into something else. That 'something else' tends to lead to unkindness.

I became curious though about the idea that kindness might be legislated. Simon believes that it can't be, but he has an interesting slant that really stuck with me:

The police will sometimes arrest someone for extreme acts of unkindness, that is, incited violence or hatred. Although on the whole I don't think it's something we can legislate out as it's something that we need to culturally change in how we see each other and how we interact with each other. I fear without the cultural change we won't change very much as it has to come from within us as a community. So to give you the only comparison I can think of: drink driving used to be perfectly acceptable as long as you don't get caught, and then as a society we decided that even if you don't get caught it is not ok as it affects other people, until there is a sea change that we decide that being unpleasant to each other just isn't on so we need to collectively come together to stop it, then that's what it's going to take.

This is also backed up by many others I spoke to who are in senior leadership roles. Non tolerance of unkindness must be adopted to see the change.

There is an interesting example in a book by Daniel Coyle called *The Culture Code*, which is fascinating because the author studied people in various categories of groups to see who was successful and why. (7) The results turned out not to be as you might expect. The 'exec' group vs the kindergarten group performed worse in problem solving within teams. This was not a one-off, it was found time and time again. Kindergarten groups also outperformed CEOs and lawyers, which seems impossible, right? However, what was found is, as adults we focus on the skills that we have and, as Coyle points out, it is the human interactions and the way people interact that is more important than the skills that they may each have, what they do as a team holds higher importance. I repeat that only because it is the basis of everything we will continue to speak about in this book:

The interaction is more important than the skills.

We spend so much time thinking about status, determining who is in charge and 'what will they will think of me', that when given a task to complete we are unable to focus on getting the task done with the best outcome. This was demonstrated in Coyle's experiment because the kindergarten group were able to work without those restraints, they took risks and offered help and guidance to each other. They were less concerned by structure but instead led by the interactions and worked together in a simple and smarter way.

I often say that my most successful personal and professional relationships make me a better person, that together while we may be only two people I would feel like we were ten. This was not down to the individuals, it was about the connection that we had and how we interacted. Interaction builds connection and this can be made to happen in any given situation which we will discuss throughout this book. A strong culture increases net income by 765% over 10 years according to a

Harvard study of 200 companies. (8) So how is that so many groups behave in a way that destroys people, but also are seen to succeed?

Three skills were seen as the key to getting a group to be the most effective culture:
1. Building safety
2. Sharing vulnerability
3. Establishing purpose

Building safety

Will Felps, who studies organisational behaviour at the University of New South Wales in Australia, conducted tests that highlighted some of the key points around building safety and its effects on the effectiveness of the group. (9)

Felps tested the effect of certain stereotypes through building 44 test groups and then placing an actor with a specific agenda into each group. Agendas included being the 'bad apple' in the group, the lazy one, the slacker and the downer. The experiment showed that the presence of such a person reduces the effectiveness of the group by 30—40%. This is consistent no matter which of these 'bad apple' roles the actor played. However, what was evident was the behaviour and the role fed into the rest of the group. They start off in high spirits and then start to adopt the behaviour of the actor. It means that their effectiveness is lowered and body language and actions are not productive. However, when the group were asked if they did well, they believed they did a good job as a group. They picked up that the task was not important. They followed the lead of the bad apple and so said to themselves that if this isn't important to you, then it is clearly not important.

However, other one group contained a person who changed the status quo. He was the part of the experiment that allowed Felps to see what the difference was. The actor was unable to penetrate this group because of this one person, who we will call John. The actor could not understand how John countered his attempt to be the 'bad apple' but it all became clear when they sat down to watch the video of the test, allowing them to analyse the behaviours and actions.

John used subtle ways and looked almost invisible. However, on investigation, it was clear that the pattern was all down to the little things. When the actor became disruptive, John would use subtle body language such as to lean towards the group. He would diffuse the situation through laughter and smiles. Felps analysed all the moves, finding that the pattern is very simple; the actor behaves in a negative way and John gives warmth. John asks open questions such as, 'What do you think of this?' or 'How would you do that?' He stayed curious. The actor said it became difficult to stay in the role and in the end just wanted to be helpful. John does not take charge, but instead creates a place for the team to grow.

Sharing vulnerability

Sharing vulnerability is something that is discussed more and more within leadership and lifestyle. Coyle says this is simply all about explaining how habits of mutual risk drive cooperating behavior. Consider the behaviours of the kindergarteners. What was observed was they had a different approach as they had no expectations and cared less about what those in the group thought of them. They were ultimately vulnerable. They had not been preconditioned by life's expectations or the limiting beliefs that time and age brings upon us.

Brené Brown is a the well-known 'shame and vulnerability researcher'. Her TED talks are a global sensation, as are her many books. From her research there is a simple outcome. Those people who live wholeheartedly, and who have great joy in their lives allow themselves to be vulnerable. (14) Not because they enjoy it per se, but because they understand it is part of the course. You need to be vulnerable to have great love; to love wholeheartedly.

Brown also highlights that we fight against being vulnerable because it is uncomfortable. She says we do this in a number of ways. Numbing – the

A Culture of Kindness

use of things such as alcohol, drugs, food and such like to deaden feelings. Perfectionism – trying to make things perfect and needing to be perfect before venturing out into the world. Foreboding joy – every time something good happens, your mind will not be able to fall into that joy and love, to be vulnerable, but simply start to think of all the things that could go wrong.

Establishing purpose

Establishing purpose is something that I hope comes across in this book as being hugely important. Everyone can refer to purpose in different ways but ultimately it is understanding why we do something as either an individual or an organisation. If the people around you don't understand your purpose, they cannot support you or the organisation, or in this instance, fit into the culture.

I like to think of purpose as a metaphorical bus ride. The leader is driving the bus. On the front of the bus the destination is written. At the bus station, an announcement tells the passengers where they can expect to stop off along the way. The route is laid out and they understand the purpose of the bus is to get from location A to location G stopping at B, C, D, E, F along the way. The purpose is clear. It doesn't matter if the bus breaks down along the way or gets a flat tyre because the passengers all understand the aim and they want to get there too, so they will help and support in getting it fixed.

If you look at the Six Seconds emotional intelligence model (10), the third section of the model is called, Give yourself. This is the idea that we give of ourselves when we lead with purpose. What is wonderful and unique about their EI model is they make purpose such a key part to success, and in this current era I think it is rightly so.

Looking at the three areas of building safety, sharing vulnerability and establishing purpose, they are all intrinsically linked. If you dive into the many theorists and researchers on each of the topics individually you will also come to the conclusion, as I have and Coyle highlights so well through his own research, they cannot exist without each other when you want to create a successful culture.

Coyle's studies found that one of the successes was the sense of family that the groups built. They saw establishing social connections as important, including close proximity, eye contact, hugs, fist pumps and handshakes. Everyone talked with everyone else and asked lots of questions. There was copious active listening, humour, thanks yous, and opening of doors. Coyle says it was addictive to be around these groups, so much so that he himself craved being in them.

In my opinion, what he talks about without really knowing it, is kindness. It's not being nice per se, rather lots of tiny acts of kindness towards one another that built a culture of success. There is a strong difference between being, 'nice' and 'kind'. Kindness is the deeper sense of niceness.

Coyle states that you don't need to be 'nice' specifically to build a strong culture. I do believe the 'warmth' displayed in Felps' experiment did build the strongest culture, demonstrating that kindness through everything is absolutely key.

Coyle also states that not talking as much allows for better results when solving problems. Connection, you would imagine, is something that only happens through meeting someone special. However, the studies discovered that this is not the case. In fact, by mimicking 'belonging cues', we can build connections. The way they measure this is through studying energy mimicry and turn taking, whether everyone talks to everyone else in the group, attention levels, voice pitch, eye contact and proximity to each other. The studies highlight that the following three areas are what is needed to establish a connection.

1. Energy - investing in the exchange at hand
2. Individualisation - treating the person as unique and valued
3. Future orientations - signaling that the relationships will continue

Hitting these key points allows the person to feel safe. Then you can go into connection mode.

We are driven by a need to be accepted to maintain our self-worth. It is a human condition and one that social media platforms recognise and exploit. We all look to be liked as this feeds our self-worth. We continually and naturally ask ourselves the following questions: 'Am I safe?' 'What is the future?', and 'Are there dangers here?'

We are naturally fearful, however, as discussed, to change a culture to one of success we must ensure safety comes first. It takes only the smallest of actions to destroy a group. But building one requires a constant flow of actions that focus on belonging cues. It is easier to burn down the house than to build it, so ensuring your group are all working on, and understanding, belonging cues is so important.

What was evident from the work of Daniel Coyle was that words are less important while actions are key to any culture being successful. It did not matter if the actions did not work, but the reaction of the group to a failure did. Just the same as the bus, to steer ourselves away from needing perfection and being ok with things not quite going as planned is ok when building a culture.

Belonging cues are plentiful, but to illustrate I have listed a few below:
Eye contact
Vocal pitch
Attention
Proximity
Inclusiveness
Energy
Mimicking
Sharing the conversation
Body language

When you receive a belonging cue, the amygdala switches roles and starts to use its immense unconscious neural horsepower to build and sustain your social bonds. It tracks members of your group, tunes in to their interactions, and sets the stage for meaningful engagement. In a heartbeat, it transforms from a growling guard dog into an energetic guide dog with a single-minded goal: to make sure you stay tightly connected with your people. On brain scans, this moment is vivid and unmistakable, as the amygdala lights up in an entirely different way. "The whole thing flips" says Jay Van Bavel, social neuroscientist at New York University. "The moment you're part of a group, the amygdala tunes in to who's in that group and starts intensely tracking them. Because these people are valuable to you. They were strangers before, but they're on your team now, and that changes the whole dynamic. It's such a powerful switch- it's a big top-down change, a total reconfiguration of the entire motivational and decision-making system. (The Culture Code) (7)

So, let's look at culture from a different point of view and how that might influence the way that people think and behave. We'll look in particular at the differences and similarities between individualistic cultures and collectivist cultures.

Individualist vs collectivist cultures

These look at the individual over the group as a whole, which may appear a selfish culture. However, in this type of culture, people are seen as independent, a culture that my mother brought me up to understand very well. In individualistic cultures it is as seen as good to be strong, self-reliant and not needing any support to get ahead in life. A few countries outside the UK that are considered individualistic cultures include the United States, Germany, Ireland, South Africa, and Australia.

Individualist cultures are very different to collectivist cultures. Collectivism stresses the importance of the group and social cooperation. Individualists are expected to survive singularly through any challenges,

A Culture of Kindness

people in collectivist cultures might be more likely to turn to family and friends for support during difficult times. People are often expected to have a more stoic point of view when things don't quite go to plan.

For individuals to focus on themselves as part of a culture, which you may say is part of city culture in many ways, has a profound effect on the way a city or country functions. With individualistic cultures preferring to focus on self, it means less human connection.

However, the collectivist culture means the community would give up everything they have for the wellbeing of the larger group, something I have seen happen in the Philippines. Whether a person is brought up in one type of culture or the other will influence their skills, how they interact in groups and workplaces and so on.

Taking a moment to look at the differences within cities and smaller country towns and villages, the cultures appear to naturally differ. Cities draw into themselves as self-sufficient individualist cultures, whereas small villages and towns will look to rely on each other for health and wellbeing support.

The effect that culture has on individual behaviour is a major topic of interest in the field of cross-cultural psychology. Cross-cultural psychologists study how different cultural factors influence individual behaviour, often focusing on things that are universal among different cultures of the world, as well as differences among societies.

One interesting phenomenon that cross-cultural psychologists have found is how people from individualist cultures describe themselves in comparison to those who are in a collectivist culture.

People from individualist societies have a mental picture about themselves, otherwise known as self-concept, that is more focused on independence rather than interdependence. As a result, they tend to describe themselves by their unique and individual personal characteristics and traits.

So, for example a person from an individualistic culture might say about themselves 'I am a problem solver, funny, and well educated.' However, someone from a person living in a collectivist society might be more likely to say something like, 'I am a good father and loyal husband.'

Just how much do these self-descriptions vary depending upon culture? Research conducted by Ma and Schoeneman (11) found that 60 percent of Kenyans (a collectivist culture) described themselves in terms of their roles within groups, while 48 percent of Americans (an individualist culture) used personal characteristics to describe themselves.

Psychologists have become more aware of the powerful influence that culture can have on individual and group behaviour.

Identity and culture
Certainly, our self-concept is an interesting topic. It delves into what makes up our personalities, and the age-old question, 'Who am I?'

Humanist psychologist, Carl Rogers approached this question by simply breaking it into three areas for us to consider when trying to understand ourselves better: (12)

1.   Self-image, or how you see yourself
Each individual's self-image is a mixture of different attributes including our physical characteristics, personality traits, and social roles. Self-image doesn't necessarily coincide with reality. Some people might have an inflated self-image of themselves, while others may perceive or exaggerate the flaws and weaknesses that others don't see.

2.   Self-esteem, or how much you value yourself

A number of factors can impact self-esteem, including how we compare ourselves to others and how others respond to us. When people respond positively to our behaviour, we are more likely to develop positive self-esteem. When we compare ourselves to others and find ourselves lacking, it can have a negative impact on our self-esteem.

3.   Ideal self, or how you wish you could be

In many cases, the way we see ourselves and how we would like to see ourselves do not quite match up.

We will share more of this as we go further into the book as I ask you to look and document some of these answers.

As we have discussed, the history of kindness has been based on the idea of moral obligation to human- and animal-kind. It is a sense of duty to ensure the survival of species. However, where does that come from in each of us? Do we all have it? It is a topic that fascinates teachers, philosophers and parents who question where does morality originate and how do we influence that?

These issues have been explored by a psychologist named Lawrence Kohlberg. Kohlberg's theory of moral development is shown (13) in six stages on three different levels. Kohlberg proposed that moral development is a continual process that occurs throughout the lifespan and not just as in childhood.

Kohlberg based his theory on a series of moral dilemmas which were presented to experimental participants. They were also interviewed to determine the reasoning behind their judgements of each scenario.

One example was 'John Steals the Drug.' In this scenario, a woman has cancer and her doctors believe only one drug might save her. This drug had been discovered by a local pharmacist and he was able to make it for $200 per dose and sell it for $2,000 per dose. The woman's husband, John, could only raise $1,000 to buy the drug. He tried to negotiate with the pharmacist for a lower price or to be extended credit to pay for it over time. But the pharmacist refused to sell it for any less or to accept partial payments. Rebuffed, John instead broke into the pharmacy and stole the drug to save his wife. Kohlberg asked, 'Should the husband have done that?'

Kohlberg was more interested in the reasoning behind the decision than whether the participant believed it to be right or wrong. He then classified the responses into various stages of reasoning, as follows.

Level 1. Pre-conventional morality
This is the earliest stage of moral development, where obedience and punishment are especially common in young children, but adults are also capable of expressing this type of reasoning. At this stage, Kohlberg says, children see rules as fixed and absolute. Obeying the rules is important because it is a means to avoiding punishment. We follow the rules and therefore if the rules are moral in nature they will be followed.

However, at this stage of moral development, children lean towards a focus on individual points of view and judge actions based on how they serve individual needs. In the 'John steals the drug dilemma', children argued that the best course of action was the choice that best served John's needs. Reciprocity is possible at this point in moral development, but only if it serves one's own interests.

Level 2. Conventional morality
This stage of moral development focuses on living up to social expectations and roles. These have changed so much over the years but still remain hugely influential. There is an emphasis on conformity, being nice, and consideration of how choices influence relationships. How we are seen by others remains high on the agenda. This stage generally aims to maintain social order. At this stage of moral development, people begin to consider society as a whole when making judgements. The focus is on

A Culture of Kindness

maintaining law and order by following the rules, doing one's duty and respecting authority.

Level 3. Post-conventional morality

The ideas of a social contract and individual rights cause people in this stage to begin to account for the differing values, opinions, and beliefs of other people. Rules of law are important for maintaining a society, but members of the society should agree upon these standards. Kohlberg's final level of moral reasoning is based on universal ethical principles and abstract reasoning. At this stage, people follow these internalised principles of justice, even if they conflict with laws and rules.

Of course, this does not cover the factors that prevent people from taking action despite the theory of why the majority might follow this in the three stages he lays out. Contributing factors such as background, social standing, mental health among others might cause someone not to act.

For the purposes of this book, this theory is an important foundation for the concept of organisational morals introduced in Chapter 4 on how we can lead with kindness.

Just before we leave this chapter we should discuss organisational culture. This refers to the values and beliefs that make an organisation, and how it feels when you enter that environment. Of course, those environments will change depending on circumstance and location if, for example, a business operates across many offices in varying locations. However, the aim for many is to always provide consistency in the 'feel' of a company. We usually aim to do this through mission statements and values that feature in any business summary or overview. However, this is insufficient to encourage the positive culture that organisations seek to drive employee engagement and, in turn, organisational growth.

Leaders need to create positive and engaging climates within organisations so that they build positive, innovative cultures. It's also true that locally positive climates encourage teams to work at a higher level. All this creates positive momentum throughout the organisation.

So, what does this evolution of organisational culture look like? I have designed a model based on a staged process of development for how we might consider changing a culture to produce success and happiness for employees and the organisation overall. We will return to this in Chapter 5 and beyond.

For now, let's look at the impact of creativity on organisational success. This is not about artistry, but rather allowing people to think and develop processes that are new and imaginative. Not having to conform to parameters set by someone else. It includes allowing people to develop solutions for how to approach a process differently. Taking the environment for example, people might consider shared spaces, larger eating areas, bigger corridors in which to have conversations. To get people up from their desks so that they will feel more motivated. Ask people to come up with ideas and then pitch them, rather than being told what they must do. Of course, we think that we don't have time for this, but I question whether any company has time not to. It means getting engagement right from the start, so encouraging a culture of trust.

It's very simple. Devoting resources and time to others and developing our softer skills rather than indulging a materialist desire, brings about lasting wellbeing and strong positive cultures.

3.1   National culture and kindness

We need to take time for each other.

Rebecca Robins, Global Chief Learning and Culture Officer, and Head
of Global Luxury Practice, Interbrand.

When I asked Emma Slade, Founder of Opening your Heart to Bhutan,
if she thought there was a divide in kindness between western and eastern
cultures, she made it clear that we must be careful with creating divisions
between any parts of the world as they are simply not comparable, each
having their own pressures and respective abilities to help others.

It got me interested in whether a particular country might be kinder than
others, and why this might be. This question is discussed within the CAF
World Giving Index, backed up by data provided through the Gallup World
Poll data (14). What it shows is that, unsurprisingly, countries vary in their
ability to give of themselves and financially based on their particular
circumstances. For example, those that are not at war or experiencing
severe political unrest remain at the top. However, what is interesting is
there is no consistency in its pattern. You might imagine that those who are
higher in the list are more economically secure, however that's not the
case. It appears to me the differences lie in the cultures at the heart of those
countries.

In 2018, Indonesia came first on the World Giving Index. Having come
second in 2017, Indonesia's three individual giving scores were largely
unchanged. However, it was because Myanmar dropped its ranking that
gave room for Indonesia.

All three of Myanmar's scores decreased since last year (donating
money is down from 91 percent to 88 percent, helping a stranger is down
from 53 percent to 40 percent and volunteering time is down by the largest
amount, from 51 percent to 34 percent). The scores for helping a stranger

and volunteering were the lowest ever recorded, which may partly be due to the Rohingya crisis as it reached its peak during 2017, (15) It is hard not to conclude that Myanmar's troubles have contributed to its people being less willing or able to give in these ways. What stayed relatively unchanged was the donation of money, but this could be in part because of strong Buddhism which requires donations to support those living a monastic lifestyle.

Two countries that entered into the top 20 this year was Singapore and Haiti, with huge improvements for both. Singapore was previously 64th just 5 years ago. Interestingly Singapore has been developing schemes to increase volunteering over recent years in the country.

Thailand had fallen from 16th place to 62nd place. It is considered that this is to do with the corruption and mismanagement of funds within donations.

The links between relative happiness and the level of giving (kindness) of a country do not seem clearly related. However, what is clear about happiness in line with kindness (or giving) is the fact that wealth and happiness are not linked. At the time of writing the nations appear to be looking at this and how mental health and happiness can be influenced.

It appears that many of the low-to-middle income countries are happier because they have more structured society and human connections. It is their only option. In contrast, those in developed countries have made their homes very cosy with many items to entertain them. They will spend time fixing, buying and using their possessions. It has become a way to bring a temporary happiness fix. In contrast, low-to-middle income countries see long-term happiness sustained through enduring connection with people and frequent human contact.

What does seem evident from the top-ranking happiest countries is they feature many Nordic countries, and the reasons appear to be a lack of

A Culture of Kindness

corruption and the fact that police and politicians are trusted. We will hear over and over that trust is a key component in how we build a successful culture.

Quoting Emma Slade once again, she highlights beautifully something that I believe helps us make a culture of kindness. While it may seem completely off topic, in fact is it hugely important in allowing a human to change their mindset regarding materialism. From this, a culture of kindness can be bred when we care less about things and more about people.

We are habitual, it is easy to cultivate a habit of believing that we ourselves are the most important. The habit of self orientation is one that can be broken. If you have enough, work out what is enough, when you get there, then you must think what will bring you joy; happiness, that will usually be about connecting to others. However, if you never feel like you have enough and you are constantly looking for more and more you probably won't ever get to that place. What is enough? This house is big enough, this car is all right. You have to weigh it up. You will never be mentally content until you have considered what enough will be.

A Culture of Kindness

4. Kindness at work

In terms of leadership, everyone is starting to recognise that in a world where we will have incredible levels of computing power, we will have machines that can replicate some form of intelligence that actually many of those human skills, and that's where I think kindness really comes into this. It's really going to stand out, and actually in our future workforce we need to pay greater attention to many of those human and social skills because they may be the most significant differentiators in a world where machines and data can report a lot of the repetitive tasks.

Sean Tompkins, Global CEO RICS

I asked several people on the podcast what they believed, from what they had seen in their work, about the effects that stress and anxiety had on the ability for humans to be kind and function in a collaborative manner. There was a general feeling that the two did not work well together as stress and anxiety were internal reactions and kindness needs a sense of external awareness.

Simon Kempton talked interestingly about this from the police force point of view. He highlighted that what you see while serving within the police can easily take its toll. For example, *there are only so many suicides you can attend before it starts to affect you.* Dani Savekar, who set up the Inspire Kindness movement says, *To choose kindness in adversity is a skill we need to be teaching ourselves.*

So, we know that we become what we feed our bodies with, that's indisputable. In a well-documented investigation, Morgan Spurlock ate Mcdonalds' food every day for 30 days to see the effects and his entire physical health as well as his mental wellbeing diminished. (16) In that same regard, I want you to also consider what we feed our minds too. All the things we see, we hear, smell and touch have a role in feeding our minds. Therefore it is clear that our environments feed us and provoke reactions.

For our emergency services, police, paramedics, fire crew and medical staff to name just a few, they have little choice in what they see and hear every day. This is where the process of building the culture of kindness that I talk about in this book works so well. We are building a culture that only positively feeds the brain and the senses.

What are the greatest leaders of kindness doing day to day? When you listen to the Culture of Kindness podcast episodes with some great leaders it is super clear that they are not doing just one act of kindness but bringing it into their day-to-day lives as a way of life. They recognise not only the benefits for themselves in the workplace, but also for their employees. They see that it benefits their health and there appears to be no other way that they believe a human can exist in total contentment without kindness.

For example, Dani Savekar said in her podcast interview, *You cannot do an act of kindness in a day and that be enough. You can't just do something and that be enough, you have to be something.* Which I believe summarises very well how we must adopt this culture.

So, let's look at some interesting research. David Rand set up his Human Cooperation Lab at Yale University (17). His laboratory is dedicated to examining the behavioural economics of niceness, so obviously he was keen to show this within his own environment. He has done this through promoting social events and creating bonds in the team that are difficult to break. Interestingly, over the years his studies have pointed to one clear takeaway; having shared responsibility is good for both individual workers and for businesses as a whole.

A Culture of Kindness

Professor Christine Porath, from University Georgetown, US, stated that through her research (18) on how people were treated in the workplace, she had seen a decline in civility. It appeared in her research that, since 1998 when a quarter of people were treated rudely at work, this figure had risen to half in 2005 and then over half in 2011. This evidence, that the way we speak to each other in the workplace in such a negative manner is rising, is something that we should be noting, because the effects of stress and pressure must surely be part of that.

Similarly, David Rand says it pays to be nice to those in the workplace. Let's say you have no scruples and no basic sense of human decency. The only thing that drives you is a desire to reach the top of a fictitious ladder. In that case, Rand talks about the idea that the one-off interactions people will be less likely to invest in. (You cut in line for the bathroom at the museum because you don't live in that town anyway—that sort of thing).

But if you're interacting with someone repeatedly, like in an office environment, it's in your best interest to be cooperative, Rand says. Usually, colleagues work together for longer than just a few days. People start to realise that if they yield to a co-worker one day, he or she will yield to them the next.

According to that theory of indirect reciprocity, others might take notice of your kindliness and form a higher opinion of you in general. This works best in environments where good behaviours are highlighted and measurements of performance are not done on financials for example. But the point remains: At work, everyone's playing a long game; the game is won by those who adopt a kindly approach to working.

Rand believes that forgiveness played an important part in this process. In one experiment, he found that people playing an unpredictable 'prisoner's dilemma' type game benefitted from forgiving their partner for acting against them. The same holds true in the business environment, which can be similarly 'noisy', as economists say. Sometimes, when it appears to us that someone is trying to undermine us, they're actually not and it is not being done intentionally. If someone doesn't credit you for something you worked hard on, you can't know whether he or she just forgot, or if it was an intentional slight. According to Rand's research, you shouldn't, say, retaliate by being quick to slight the person to others. Losing those relationships and connections over what can be a simple mistake can be a costly one in the long term.

In Rand's studies, *the strategy that earns the most money is giving someone a pass and letting the person take advantage of you two or three times.* Our natural tendency is to go against this and immediately react, rather than talk or let things slide. Rand also completed a study about how we treat people. Being fair and generous was the better stance to take, his conclusion: '*In an uncertain world, fairness finishes first.*'

Lord Mark Price, Founder of Engaging Works, former Deputy Chairman of The John Lewis Partnership and Managing Director of Waitrose., wrote a book on exactly this topic, entitled *Fairness for all: Unlocking the power of employee engagement.* (19) In it he highlights the six ways to treat employees fairly based and adapted from his 34 years in the John Lewis Group in which he embodied exactly that. It starts with six key factors; reward and recognition, information sharing, empowerment, wellbeing, instilling pride and job satisfaction. He talks about paying people fairly, highlighting that while it is not the totality, *None of this is to say we can ignore pay altogether. Pay is a key concern for everyone and if you are not paying a fair salary no amount of recognition for a job well done will be enough to make your employees forget they are not being paid enough.* He highlights that in fact other main contributing factors are good leadership, low stress, clear goals from an individual perspective and business. In other words, managers who coach and are consistent improve the company image.

Organisations are seeking out leaders with the softer skills, ones that can be intuitive and care about their people.

In a 2014 leadership (20) survey, the PR firm Ketchum wrote that *there's a "seismic move away from an outdated, 'macho' model of solitary leadership—a command-and-control approach centered on one-way rhetoric, obsessively controlled messaging and solitary decision-making—and towards a new, more 'feminine' archetype.* Though respondents to the survey still said they preferred male leaders by a slight margin (54 percent to 46 percent), they also said that women possessed more of the individual leadership characteristics they desired, like bringing out the best in others and being transparent. Women came out on top on 10 of the 14 leadership attributes the firm examined.

In Fred Kiel's book *Return on Character*, (21) found that people worked harder and more happily when they felt valued and respected. He found that CEOs who possessed four virtues—integrity, compassion, forgiveness, and accountability—lead companies whose returns on assets are five times larger than those of executives who were more self-centred.

Harvard Business School's Amy Cuddy and her research partners have also shown (22) that leaders who focus on showing warmth rather than skills and strength first are more effective. Why? It comes down to trust. Employees feel greater trust in someone who is kind. This has also been backed up by many of the Culture of Kindness podcast interviews I have conducted with CEOs, in which interviewees say that they believe trust to be key.

In her interview Pippa Richardson, HR consultant, shared a wonderful example of how a kind leader can gain the greatest wins. She was working for a company that was about to undergo a national organisational change, so a roadshow had been set up to explain the changes to employees. This was not an easy conversation to be had as some had worked for the high street bank for many years and were due to be moved over by TUPE (Transfer of Undertakings and Protection of Employment) to the new owner. Some had worked there for decades, including whole families who saw it was a job for life. What they were going to experience was immense emotionally. The plan was to deliver this over three locations, one in the north of England, then fly south to deliver the same message. Pippa recalls the moment that snowy conditions had stopped the flights the night before they were due to fly. Pippa called the director in charge of delivering the message and asked what was the back-up plan? She suggested that for safety they might have to postpone. However, this particular director decided it was too important. He organised a hire car and drove in the early hours of the morning to get there. He was a little late but the staff were made to feel valued, to feel that they were cared for on a whole different level. So much so it started a ripple throughout the process. *It went viral. Someone had put themselves out to deliver the message, you could feel the calm over the workforce, he demonstrated through his actions that he cared. Everyone started wanting to help. Everyone was communicating and explaining, helping managers get things done, the hairs on my arm have risen just thinking about it and remembering being part of that energy.*

A Culture of Kindness

4.1   Challenges faced

We end up more disconnected and less empathic than we have ever been. Look at Twitter or read any anonymous comments section, these spaces dehumanize us and give disproportionate power to the angriest voices. The more that's seen to be normal, the more we separate from each other. I worry about the impact that this will have on our collective empathy. Social media clearly creates a dissonance in us individually. If we communicated face to face with the same anger and vitriol, we reserve for social media we'd be eaten by guilt and shame. However, if this lack of empathy ends up being a more widespread cultural thing rather than an individual action then how does that impact on us as a species? If that sort of angry rhetoric is normalized and we all retreat further into misanthropic solipsism how will that effect our reaction to big global problems like human rights abuse, famine, war or ecological crisis? We are chipping away at our humanity in such subtle increments that it's almost imperceptible.

Byron Vincent, Writer, performer and broadcaster

Social media

Social media has obviously had an effect on the way we live and interact. It was designed for many reasons but mainly to bring users together in larger numbers than ever before. You never need to lose contact with anyone or miss someone getting married, having a child, splitting up or even dying. You can know it all in the palm of your hand. Which can bring with it waves of support from people; you would hope. This is where social media is at odds with itself. As much as we would all like to believe we are drawn to the wonderful stories, as humans our default is to be drawn to the drama and scandal.

Why you might imagine would we do that?, asks Adam Phillips' book, *Missing out, in praise of the unlived life.* (23) He highlights that depression, anxiety and negative emotions are a result of living a life of dissatisfaction. Social media feeds this as we compare our lives with others based on one-dimensional snapshots. Johann Hari also talks about the 'unmet needs' of the human being the key to why depression is prevalent. (24) According to Phillips, scandal allows us to live a life that is sexier, richer, daring or anyway different from our own, hence causing the life of dissatisfaction.

Scandal for me though, can also give a person a sense that they are not the only one getting it wrong sometimes. We are our own worst critics, even the most stoically positive person will have moments of self-doubt, or make a mistake that if they had their chance again would do differently. Scandal gives us an opportunity to beat someone else up rather than ourselves.

By causing such a range of emotions that are often unpredictable, scandal allows us to have those emotions outside of ourselves rather than them being about ourselves, and that's what makes it something that we are always drawn to. The issue with that is that the algorithms of social media know that. Social media is growing all by itself. AI is far beyond anything we can control within our current policy and legislative frameworks. The marketers and the advertisers understand it and it has become propaganda for consumerism and therefore the human condition.

Although Benjamin Mathes, founder of Urban confessional, the free listening movement, has a more positive take on it when I interviewed him for the Culture of Kindness podcast:

I wonder what is going to happen as some people use social media so beautifully to connect, but it is different from that communion we can connect to. I wonder where the tipping point will be. In the last ten years since the phone came out it has new technology that has almost simultaneously made us addicted to screens but also heightened our awareness of our lack of person-to-person connection. It's almost as if everywhere I go people crave to be with each other so badly that it happens, in spite of all of it.

He appears to be right, as shown by the rising up from the sidelines of those who want their data back from Silicon Valley as they get rich on manipulation of our minds. People want something of history, to be human and not to be controlled anymore.

Simon Kempton has this to say on it:

Social media has had a massive difference in the way we communicate. I'd knock about with my mates when I joined the army and was a kid, we'd go hang out, go play footy and the social circle was relatively small. Whereas now people are in much larger groups, but these are not face-to-face groups so it's much easier to be unpleasant to someone. When you grew up in your formative years face to face you had to learn how to be kind or you wouldn't have any friends. In social media, you can be unkind, get blocked and you can move on to someone else. You can keep moving on and never run out of people to be unkind to with the 25 million Snapchat users.

We have lost something in learnt interpersonal skills that you learnt naturally if you didn't want to be alone 20 years ago, I am not sure of what the answer is.

One possible answer lies in the Conclusion to this book, well for the workplace anyway. The way we conduct performance reviews has to be based on the softer skills and how people can look to develop themselves. Any effort to do this in and outside of work for the greater good of humanity should be rewarded accordingly.

Mental Health

When we talk about empowering people in poverty, I think a large part of the conversation has to be focused around stress and anxiety. Those two things impact everything from diet to our capacity to empathise. The immediate comfort of junk food or alcohol seems much more appealing if you're in a constant state of stress. It's hard for us to be present and nurturing when we're anxious. Stress inhibits our ability to build strong relationships and reduces our capacity for kindness, this means that people who are suffering economic stresses will also likely suffer emotional stress.

I think a lot of the developments that occurred in the latter half of the 20th century have contributed to a general decline in Mental Health. Communities were fractured and isolated by the death of traditional industry and rapidly advancing technologies. Industrialised food production and retail made us less active and introduced unhealthy synthetic foods into our diets. Convenience has made us less active and our bodies are less driven to produce hormones that keep our mental health in natural good order. Media and marketers started using guilt, shame and desire to make us more motivated consumers. These things have all had a negative impact.

Byron Vincent, Writer, performer and broadcaster

We need several things to have strong mental health. We need a sense of purpose, a good sense of self, an ability to work on emotional intelligence, exercise, good food and to be feeding the senses with positive and healthy things, such as the environment in which we live.

Now you would imagine that this should be simple, it's easy for anyone to do those things when they are listed out like that. However, the world we live in does not lend itself to that. Consumerism has had a major effect. Companies need to sell things, so we are fed advertising that affects our mental health. We have become sensitized to how a person looks, what they have and the comparison culture of, 'What I don't have' to name a few. It feeds the gremlins of envy as we aspire to be like them and buy all the products to achieve this. It follows us into the workplace and our overall lives. We are consistently and subconsciously affected by the sheer volume of stimuli that we are now exposed to.

A Culture of Kindness

Social media is the latest way to drug ourselves from lives we are not happy with. However, many think that it actually makes us even unhappier when we get caught in the 'Scroll spiral'. You are scrolling through the social media feeds. The scroll spiral, as I like to refer to it, is the one that you don't know you are in until five minutes into it and you are so far down you struggle to stop. Your brain has been fed in that five minutes, depending on the algorithms that your feed gives you, a sea of adverts and people sharing either drama or the perfect life and the odd cat video.

Twenty-five percent of the UK suffers with a mental health disorder each year, with approximately twenty percent in the US experiencing just stress and anxiety. (25) However, just a hundred years ago during World Wars One and Two, life was at the extremes of love and loss, yet people did not report mental health issues, maybe this was due to the lack of conversation about it, access to resources and also maybe the stigma that we have spent the past ten years trying to remove. It was a time when you stayed married through thick and thin. Food was rationed and the comfort we now see in homes did not exist. Life was simpler and what was a luxury, such as imported fruit for example, is a given now.

Pressure to be something great is much larger in this present day. Before it was about survival; 'putting food on the table', was the saying. Everyone had a place in the world and even if you didn't like it you got on with it because to step out of those expectations and daily routines was considered ungodly.

We are, by comparison, free to do as we please. Those who don't are really only constrained by their own minds. However, enabled by technology, we have revisited the consumerism of the 1920s that saw people buying things that they didn't need. We now fill our lives with more 'things' than anyone before. It has for some become a form of numbing addiction to the struggles that people see in their own self confidence.

Generational differences

Sally Waterston is the joint non-exec chair of the successful company Waterstons that she set up in 1994 with two others, including her husband. She believes that we have a lot to learn from generational differences, and that reverse mentoring is one of the keys to great leadership: *You need to take on people who are cleverer than you.*

Our generational differences are deemed so large that we have even named them. They are dictated by economists, politicians and social climate generally. Populations have grown and the world has advanced so much so that we have to name groups of people to understand their dynamics. This was once called prejudice, but here it is seen as a way to better understand why one person doesn't understand another's point of view. There is some contradiction there if you really think about it for everything we are constantly fighting against.

We only started naming generations in the 19th century, and the gaps between the generations seems to have changed dramatically since. The age ranges also appear to vary depending on the country. However, what is clear is that the gap between the generations seems to shorten. Baby boomers and the silent generation before them were similar, there was a sense of general understanding between them. By comparison, baby boomers and millennials see life's challenges very differently. We are developing faster than ever before, and it takes time for us to really understand the impact of those changes. The ways we interact, understand and mentor have never had to be so diverse. To find success we must as humans be the most open-minded we have ever been to be effective and harmonious.

Ideas on generational differences vary greatly, including on how to name them. This example taken from 'Socialchange.co.uk' (26) written by Emily Rose was the best example and most thoroughly researched I came across that gave sufficient depth for this book. It not only seemed the most relevant, but also gave leaders a chance to understand better how to support their teams comprising multiple generations. To make sure which of these generations your teams have been shaped by is as important as personality profiling or similar.

The generation discussion goes something like this.
"You don't understand what it was like when I was growing up."
"Your generation gets it all handed to you these days."
"My generation are paying for your generation's mistakes."
"When I was your age, we didn't have all the opportunities you have."

We've heard all of these many times I'm sure. I'm also sure that it doesn't matter what generation you are, your parents and grandparents will always tell you how easy you have it and how your generation don't have the same values and ethic as their generation. It seems that without us really knowing, we have been put into a 'generation box'. And apparently all those in that box share the same attitudes, values and habits, shaped by the world we grew up in. I've taken a look at the different generations to see if when we were born says something about who we really are.

The SILENT GENERATION (Born 1925-1945)

For those still alive, the silent generation exhibit more conservative views than the generations which follow. Their childhood and youth were shaped by war and economic depressions, but fortunately enjoyed almost full employment and prosperity in their later life with the economic boom. They believe in hard work and have a waste-not, want-not mentality. They are the first generation to see the class system begin to break down and contemplated an early retirement.
World events: World War II, the Great Depression, Creation of NHS
Cultural influences: George Orwell, Orson Wells, Gone with the Wind
Technology: Technicolour films, Radio

Economics: The great depression caused a world-wide financial crisis in the 30s and the 40s and they were crippled by war and post war debt. This generation experienced rationing and little to no disposable income. This would continue until the post war economic boom of the 1950s.

As consumers: Despite coming into prosperity in their later life, benefitting from the housing boom and large pension payouts, this generation are not large spenders. Although a number of them do use a computer, they are not likely to make a purchase online or pay attention to ads preferring traditional methods of marketing.

The BABY BOOMERS (Born 1945-1963)

The 'Baby Boomers' refers to the children born during the period following World War II when birth rates were high and the economy was improving. Most born during this period will be at retirement age now, or in a senior position in their jobs nearing retirement. They represent the largest and most affluent market in history - they were too young to have a personal memory of the immediate aftermath of the war, but old enough to remember the post war high. They are known for their work ethic (influenced by the silent majority), loyalty and they are very focused on their professional lives.

World events: The assassination of JFK, the Cold War, the Vietnam War, the Moon Landing, Korean War.

Cultural influences: The Beatles, Rock n Roll, John Wayne, Economic Migrants from the Commonwealth, Sexual revolution.

Technology: Television and telephones in the majority of households.

Economics: Generally considered to be the wealthiest generation due to growing up in a period of post war government subsidiaries. In 2004, the UK Baby-Boomers held 80% of the UK's wealth.

As consumers: Baby Boomers are more likely to be loyal to a particular brand than the younger generations. They are also more likely to make a purchase based on the object's value.

A Culture of Kindness

GENERATION X (Born 1964-1974)

The introduction of the contraceptive pill in the early 1960s was a huge factor in the lower birth rates of generation X , or the "baby busters" as they are occasionally referred to as. As individuals, they are known for being nihilistic and cynical, and this is certainly understandable considering that they came of age just in time to experience Thatcherism, a series of economic crises, and the AIDS epidemic, just to name a few. They were born into a time where the adult experience was valued over the child experience, divorce rates were high and both parents tended to be in full time work. They are known as the latchkey children, as they lacked adult supervision in the hours between the end of school and the time their parents returned home from work, leading them to be largely independent and self managing.

World events: Thatcherism, the AIDs 'crisis', the fall of the Berlin wall, Band Aid

Cultural influences: Punk, indie movies, mod culture

Technology: Multiple channel television and video players were introduced during their adolescence. The internet was introduced, however it was not widely available until the 1990s, so most had no experience with it until then.

Economics: They grew up through the tough financial times of the late 1980s, but experienced the housing and technology boom when they began to enter the workforce. They hold the highest employment rate of any demographic.

As consumers: Generation X pride themselves on making informed purchasing decisions and will now turn to the Internet to research products. They are less likely to compare brand in search for value for money - they have been shown to spend extra on brands they know and trust. Marketers have struggled to reach this generation, but they have been shown to adapt to new technology, now doing banking and shopping online (despite being a teenager and young adult in the days when banking was done face to face in a bank).

A Culture of Kindness

XENNIALS (born 1975-1983)

The Xennial generation is a 'new micro generation' that has recently been coined to refer to those who were born during a period where they do not fit the typical definitions of Generation X or Millennials. People born between 1975 and 1983 were exposed to an analogue adolescence but a digital adulthood. This is the generation often referred to as the last generation of children to play outdoors. As this is a newly created generation category, there is not much data available yet. They are said to be the generation which bridges the gap between Generation X and the Millennials, possessing much of the work ethic associated with Gen X, but with the optimism of the Millennials.

World events which shaped their upbringing: The fall of the Berlin wall, Death of Princess Diana, World Wide Web open to the public, the end of Apartheid.

Pop culture influences: Britpop (Oasis vs Blur), Friends, rave scene, Ministry of Sound

Technology: World Wide Web, email, AOL, cable for television were all defining factors for Xennials in terms of technology. They are typically more tech savvy than Generation X, adapting to major technological change within their lifetimes. As social media became popular whilst they were in their 20s, they managed to avoid the cyberbullying and sexting pressures that later generations faced.

Economics: This generation got their careers underway before the economic crash of 2008. They benefitted from tuition-free higher education or low tuition fees, meaning they entered the workforce with considerably less debt than those just a few years younger.

As consumers: Xennials are tricky to pin down, as they essentially have one foot in the analogue and one foot in the digital. Xennials are a progressive generation in terms of social and cultural views, so they don't respond as well to traditional marketing methods as their predecessors.

　　　　　　　　　　　　　A Culture of Kindness

The MILLENNIALS (born 1984-1995)

Millennials (often referred to as Generation Y) possesses many characteristics that are unique in comparison to past generations. They tend to value job satisfaction and fulfilment over wages, they prefer a non-authoritative approach in the workplace and have a preference for immediate feedback. They are more tech savvy than previous generations, leading to a reputation for being self-absorbed and narcissistic. They are also widely viewed as optimistic and progressive on cultural and social values.

World events which shaped their upbringing: 9/11 terrorist attacks, the credit crunch, the war in Iraq, boxing day Tsunami

Cultural influences: The Harry Potter Books, Spice Girls, Reality TV

Technology: Although they will remember dial-up connection and a time without mobile phones, the majority of their adolescence and young adulthood would have been spent online and they would remember the birth of social media.

Economics: A combination of national debt, globalisation, lack of jobs, rising house prices and lower incomes, the Millennials are said to be the first generation to be worse off than the previous generation.

As consumers: According to research by Inkling, 60% of UK Millennials will engage with online content that interests them, even if it's obvious that it's been paid for by a brand. They have been shown to be more likely to be influenced by reviews and blogs as opposed to ads. 78% have said they would rather have a desirable experience over a desirable product.

GENERATION Z (born 1996-2010)

Whilst we don't know much about Gen Z yet, the oldest of the generation being 22 at the moment, we know a lot about the environment they are growing up in. Known as the first 'tech natives', they were born into a highly sophisticated media and computer environment and due to this they have been labeled "screen addicts". Typically, they have shorter attention spans, due to the rise of videos and easy access information. With the rise of social media and the ability to connect with anyone around the world, they value personal engagement and transparency in companies and brands, something businesses and organisations are needing to adapt to.

World events which shaped (or are currently shaping) their upbringing: Syrian refugee crisis, Legalisation of gay marriage, Trump politics

Cultural influences: London Olympics, social media, online streaming

Technology: The tech revolution has had the biggest impact on Generation Z. Unlike previous generations, they were born into rapid technology advances. They're the first generation to be spending longer online on their mobiles each day than on all other devices combined.

Economics: The rise in university tuition fees has resulted in less of this generation seeking out higher education and seeking employment instead. It is predicted that, like the millennials, they will feel the strain of high housing prices.

As consumers: Generation Z are the least likely generation to remain loyal to a particular brand. They prefer their brands to reach them on social media, and are more inclined to buy products online as opposed to going to a shop. Gen Zers are also expanding on the idea, often attributed to millennials, of wanting to buy brands that stand for something. They definitely want to make the world a better place and now they have the technology to do so.

Visual storytelling matters too. Older millennials might spend time cropping photos, picking the right filters and choosing the right images to show their best selves, But for Gen Z, this is not cool at all.

And while there are plenty of risks in having influencers promote brands, influencers have a more direct approach that resonates with the people who follow them on Instagram, YouTube and elsewhere.

A Culture of Kindness

What Emily Rose has done here is a give a complete guide that I believe should be referenced back to as her detail is extremely useful for your ongoing understanding.

I asked many of my interviewees how they believe generational difference impacts kindness and many of them consider kindness as coming from a willingness to understand which is in itself being kind. I particularly liked Simon Kempton's take on this:

There is a stereotype or cliché, like most if you listen to stereotype there is kernel of truth behind them. Which if you read certain papers that there are gangs of feral youths hanging around the streets waiting to stab you. But I've got some real optimism about the next generation, my daughter's generation. When you look at how 16/17 year-olds tackled the Scottish referendum debate, some of the most mature thoughts came from that age group. If you look at Brexit, some of the most salient points are coming from young adults and youngsters. That generation is far more accepting, tolerant of difference, outward looking and aware of equality issues. Far less likely to raise an eyebrow because someone is transgender or gay. Far more likely to reach out to strangers. I see a lot on Twitter who are clearly damaged and talking about themselves and people are reaching out to them, and I find that quite heartwarming. Again, going back to the random act of kindness to and from strangers, I have quite a lot of optimism in general about the next generation, but I feel we may leave them a planet that is beyond repair. Our generation and our parents need to consider how we lead our lives.

The message is clear, there is hope for the world with our younger generations stepping into the fold.

Capitalism

Looking back to Emma Slade's quote, the Founder of 'Opening your heart to Bhutan', she asks, when is enough, enough, when it comes to the things you own in your life. It becomes the beating heart of capitalism and how to control our own spending so as to not affect the our connections with fellow humans.

Byron Vincent, writer, performer and broadcaster also has an opinion on how our empathy and kindness is affected by capitalism.

It is detrimental to our self image. 15 years ago we were rightly concerned about magazines photoshopping models into impossible physical archetypes. These days with face editing apps we do it to ourselves. Throughout history the things we've arbitrarily decided are attractive have always veered towards the ridiculous; powdered wigs and hobble skirts spring to mind. Now we have snapchat filters that give us animated dog ears and eyes the size of tennis balls. Really these arbitrary aesthetics have nothing to do with beauty. We're bombarded with imagery and media that deliberately exploits our neuroses and desire to belong. If we just adorn ourselves in the right product we'll be better, happier people. In reality these arbitrary aesthetic fads pull time and focus away from genuine self improvement and if anything make us more neurotic and less able to function as decent, kind and empathetic people.

Capitalism was seen by some as an answer to how to bring ourselves out of poverty and grow the economy, however many saw that it might just have the power to destroy much about the best parts of human connection. People continually refer to the rich getting richer. As Lord Price highlights in his book *Fairness for All*, Oxfam's 2015 global inequality report says that the top 62 wealthiest people in the world own as much as over half of the world's population put together. Just 5 years previously it had been 368 people. And top executives who earned 47 times more than their average employees around 20 years ago now earn 183 times more. The facts are staring at us in the face.

Lord Price also says, *I believe more than ever that capitalism needs a different approach, a kinder, more thoughtful, tolerant, patient, engaging and inclusive approach. It needs to embrace the many, not the few, if we are going to survive as the world's prevalent economic force, and it needs to consider and weigh up carefully its long-term effects on future generations.* In my opinion, he is right. For example, what capitalism has done to our environment will have an effect so large we are only just starting to see its some of its lighter ripples, the tsunami is yet to be released.

Let's take plastic, waste and pollution. The obvious effects are the pollution of our seas and harm to wildlife. But there are also the micro plastics that are entering our body through our foods and the air we breathe, plastics we were never designed to ingest. The effects on the body of this are unknown. This is a one example of the effects of capitalism, our need as humans for more 'things'.

My mother remembers when they moved to the town in which they still live. There was a greengrocers, you would take your cloth bag or wicker basket and you would ask through the door for the fruit and veg you wanted. They would weigh it out and pour it into your chosen carrier. No plastic bags, just produce. Whether we like it or not, capitalism has brought out the very worst parts of us as humans. The desire to fill our lives and homes with things has stopped us from caring about our neighbours. We have set up processes to obtain all these things without having to deal with people, internet shopping to name just one, in fact it's so easy we never need leave our homes at all.

A Culture of Kindness

4.2   How to make a successful organisation based on kindness

In the '80s and '90s we used to lead from the front and now we lead from behind and that's quite a transition.

Sean Tompkins, Global CEO, RICS

Leadership has evolved so much and, while some are still stuck in the 1980s and 1990s, those who are seeing longevity and healthy growth are those who recognise that human connection, kindness and trust are the only ways to lead.

Most businesses focus on their missions and objectives, which are of course important and have a place. However, more often than not they are no more than words, and in reality, feel corporate and distant. This means they are not adhered to and in time become a mockery for the disgruntled employee. Because mission statements primarily relate to the company and not the employee, it becomes challenging to build a culture around the ideology they contain.

It helps to imagine building a culture of kindness as if you were building a house.

Imagine the key components of a house. Firstly you will always need a strong foundation. Without this, your house will start to crack and eventually fall down. Once you have your foundations you will need to build the walls. The walls will keep in place everything else. You'll have doors and windows of course and then your roof to keep everyone dry and warm. So let's build your house.

The foundations

This part is building safety within a culture. It gives people a solid foundation of knowing the rules they need to follow which is reassuring. Organisational morals make up the foundation. You will find also if you do the course that supports this book that vision, mission and purpose are equally important, however for this part we focus on the organisational morals and how to develop them to make your culture.

Walls
You've got four walls. These relate to the four levels of emotional intelligence. We need to build not only our own emotional intelligence, but that of the teams or groups you are aiming to build this culture within. This part is about being true to yourself, sharing vulnerabilities and understanding the people around you. The four walls are, Self Awareness, Self Management, Social Awareness, Relationship Management.

Roof
This last piece cannot be started without doing the other work, otherwise it will have nothing to keep it up. It relates to values development and establishing purpose. In the culture of kindness theory there are seven values to focus on.

Organisational morals

Morals *plural*
a: Moral practices or teachings: modes of conduct an authoritative code of ***morals*** has force and effect when it expresses the settled customs of a stable society – Walter Lippmann
Merriam Webster Dictionary

So, let's start by considering the foundation of this house, which is likely to be very safe once you have finished it.

I cannot start without mentioning Tom Levitt, who is a guest on the podcast and author of *The Company Citizen: Good for Business, Planet, Nation and Community* and his thoughts on the need for companies to start defining their purpose for why they exist. We have to start to think about it as more than just making money.

Why does your company exist? Ensuring that purpose is prevalent will allow the rest of the house to grow through to building the culture with ease.

It's now time to talk about which behaviours are accepted or not within an organisation. Although this can be sporadic, when we employ people it is so much easier to measure whether a person will fit into your culture by using behaviours and personality profiling to match the organisation's purpose.

Having 'rules' may seem a little harsh, but to build a culture we must have a list of what is acceptable as discussed previously. For the ongoing purpose of this theory we will be calling the items on this list **morals**. Morals have consistently throughout history been the cornerstone of kindness.

Your organisation should define a set of morals that they have developed in a structured team setting. This development process should include people from all levels of the business in a five-stage process.

Emotional intelligence testing
You will gather a collection of people who score highly on the EQ (Emotional Quotient) test (above 80 percent would be preferable). If you prefer you can include some with a lower score and get them to complete the activities as laid out in this book and the Culture of Kindness course available on the website. This should raise EQ significantly enough to contribute well to the next exercise (You can go to www.nahlasummers.com to complete an EQ test for free. Also see Chapter 5a.3 for more on EQ).

The reason that raising EQ levels is important for group activities is it allows you to be secure that they will be aware of other employees, working well in a team environment to ensure the outcome is something that can be managed in the business as a whole not just for the few.

Build a team of approximately six-to-ten employees from various areas of the business, such as helpdesk, finance, HR, operations, leadership, health and safety, among others. The person with the highest EQ score should lead the team in the following activity.

They will go through an exercise of forming a focus group of the employees to draw out the organisational morals by looking at what the organisation does well, and what it does less well. As a group, the team should look at wellbeing and happiness surveys data (see the Appendices for advice on obtaining this). Also, ensure that the employees from the team are going back to their peers and asking questions to encourage open and honest feedback about how they feel about work day to day.

Once all this data has been gathered, developed and discussed in a series of structured focus group meetings, it is time to start pulling out the organisational morals.

The development of the organisational morals should address the issues facing the organisation. For example, if there are high stress levels, consideration should not be directed toward simply installing a gym in the building. Instead, the focus should be on determining where that stress is coming from precisely. Is it because they feel that they are not listened to? Is it because they are overloaded with work because someone else is not pulling their weight, or that the saturation of workload is not being proactively and equally distributed among the staff?

Before I give you a list of examples to use, I'd like to cite Sally Waterston again for her brilliant and successful way of utilising trust as a value. By so doing they made a rare and unexpected rule and have a happy workforce as a result. They believed when they set up the company that everyone has a life outside of work, so created a system whereby people

A Culture of Kindness

do not 'clock in, clock out'. She believes you have to trust people to get the best out of them (trust is discussed in the upcoming chapters).

We've never had fixed hours and never had fixed holidays. We acknowledge people have a life outside of the business that is more important than the business. People told us we would never make a profit and that people would take advantage of us. But we have made a profit and grown every year. We have a very loyal workforce because we understand they have a life outside of work.

The organisational morals are not about military-style rules, for example that you come in at 9am and leave at 5pm, and you can't do fewer hours but we welcome it if you do more. No longer is the following statement acceptable, 'In our office it's an unsaid cultural position to see who will clock up the most hours.' No! Those times are long gone folks. This is why we are the least productive country as highlighted in the Financial Times, (27) everyone is just so darn tired.

To provide some clearer ideas on what organisational morals can or could consist of, I have listed the following and will go into these in more detail as we progress through the chapters.

We never blame anyone
Blame is the killer of all things. When we say its 'not my fault, it's yours' there is nowhere to go from there that is positive. The person is made to feel bad and/or they will retaliate with either more blame or remorse.

When someone is struggling we make sure we show support towards that person
Often within a workplace people feel isolated because they may not be performing as well as they would like, or at the level the company expects. To this I always say, as do top CEOs with a kindness approach to

leadership, 'No one goes to work wanting to do a bad job'. There is no point in beating someone up for not doing a good job, if they aren't achieving you need to change instruction or look at different tasks or improve your training or communication. There are a thousand things we can deliver differently to get better outcomes from others.

We always say thank you

It does not matter if it wasn't quite what you expected or for some reason you don't quite gel with the person. Thank you should be in every organisational morals list. Thank you for your time. Thank you for your support. Thank you for your commitment. What you should decide within a focus group is how that thanks will be given beyond the everyday exchanges between colleagues and groups. So, will you send thank you cards, birthday cards, appreciation post-its? Whatever you do, be creative but make sure it will last the test of time. That whatever you do, you reinvent it each year or embed a solid action that allows people to easily live by the organisational morals.

We own our mistakes

Being able to say sorry is important in this world. However, making sure that when you say sorry you also say you caveat it with the reason why.

For example:

'I am sorry as I my words were not intended to make you feel that way, the reason I responded like that was because I was in a hurry and didn't think through my choice of words.'

'I am sorry that didn't achieve what I wanted it to, although I did put a lot of effort in and maybe you could give me some feedback on what you suggest'.

These are conversations that we aren't often having. They are what I call, 'whole statements' as they contain the whole picture of the event that has caused upset. We can in one sentence like this own a mistake and allow a positive way forward. Whole statements are so important.

We show appreciation for a person's strengths

It is easy for teams to focus on the things that don't work, or the people who are not bringing the expected results. However, the more you focus on strengths, the more the weaknesses will take care of themselves. That is a basic moral, be kind to people about their strengths.

On a deeper level, we make people do work that their brains are simply not equipped to focus on. For example, some people are good with numbers and some with design. You wouldn't ask an artist to necessarily do the accounts and you should always think this way right down to individual tasks. Play to the strengths of the individual, it will make them feel better and it will also increase productivity.

We complete an act of kindness everyday

Kindness extends life, helps our health physically and mentally (3) and provides support to humanity as a whole. This organisational moral is a no-brainer. It is key to promoting all the other organisational morals that you will set. It promotes a mindset of trust and all the other values that we will discuss, and which are essential for successful business. This is such a great foundation on which all the rest of the house can firmly stand.

Trust starts with you, you manage your own time

Working environment matters. Really it matters, not what you like or your boss likes, but where your staff feel comfortable to work and feel inspired and motivated. That might mean the staff member chooses to work in the café down the street for the day or at home or from a client's offices. They need to be empowered to manage their own environment without judgement or retribution. It might be that they choose to sit in the park, why not when we know that our external environment has huge benefits to our mental wellbeing? There are so many organisational morals that you can design that start around building trust within the culture.

You will not work when there are family events happening

Many of us with family caring responsibilities already put a huge amount of guilt on themselves for attempting to have a life outside of work. If I asked for a show of hands, it would be a full house no doubt. No organisation needs to add to that. The work-hard/play-hard mentality, while reduced, is still going strong in many workplaces, leading to burn out, stress, high staff turnover and other HR issues. If you don't put your employees' personal lives first they won't put you first. Be kind to them, they will be kind back.

We all commit to working on our own emotional intelligence

Emotional intelligence is not a one-time deal. It needs to be constantly promoted, and to continually evolve. This is not simply for the benefit of the organisation when people are dealing with problem solving and team work, but also for general wellbeing. When a person becomes more self-aware they are far better able to deal with the challenges of life and daily stresses. You owe it to your staff to place emotional intelligence somewhere in your organisational morals.

The above outline what you could offer and, of course, they are good foundations, but adapt and expand them to make them work for your workplace for the wellbeing of your staff. This will ensure that you have a robust foundation on which to build the house of cultural kindness.

A Culture of Kindness

5. How to lead with kindness

5a.1   You first

Not everyone will get what I mean by this, but to build the walls of the house you must focus on 'you' first. It feels like it goes against the whole idea of kindness but in fact it is the only way. This is true for all the people who talk about the servant leader. The idea is that the leader must be there to serve others first. While it will become clear in this book that style has a place in this theory, you have to first be a health leader to support others.

Think of the age-old story of the aeroplane emergency. When you board a plane and the crew run through the emergency procedure, they always advise you to put the oxygen on yourself before you help someone else. It applies to all life's emergencies, the things that are sent to test us and challenge our abilities. If you are not equipped to deal with the challenge, how can you help someone else?

You must do the work on yourself to know who you are. It's not a job that can be done once and then ticked off the list, it's a constant evolution. It also is not, 'I need to be perfect before I can support others'. It's exactly the opposite in fact. You simply need to understand who you are so you can show up for the people you work with and really be a positive asset to the team. We all have things about ourselves that need some work, identifying them though is often the most challenging thing. Once you can own who you are, the actions you need to follow to improve fall into place.

Let's consider an example. Say I spend the time to do a personality profile test, in fact I do several of them. I read them and start to highlight and extract the commonalities. I ask friends for feedback through a structured questionnaire, and do the same for people I worked with, including both those I worked well with and those that were less compatible. I test my Emotional Intelligence, highlighting my weaker areas, and I also look at my general health, including what I eat and drink over the course of a week.

From that I discover that:

- My relationship management score on my Emotional Intelligence test is far lower than I had expected.
- I have a strong character with a driven outlook.
- My diet includes really high levels of sugar.

For brevity, we'll just look at these three examples.

1. At this stage I would be able to understand that I need to work on building better relationships. I would look at factors in my life that could be limiting my ability to improve that. I may also decide to do an Emotional Intelligence course to develop it and practice daily exercises to help with that.

2. I am pretty driven. This finding is hugely important when developing others and building working relationships. For example, someone who is quieter might find my demeanour intimidating. Therefore, discussing this openly and being able to share character traits is important to flag in teamwork. Obviously, this needs to be done in a positive way that does not belittle another.

3. Diet is really important and we will talk about that in Chapter 5a.2. Note that it does affect your ability to do your work in the most productive way and how you feel about yourself. We are truly what we eat so, if you want to be a great team player and high performer, food intake really does matter.

The above are only a few examples, but there are plentiful other areas for developing yourself as an instrument of kindness in the workplace.

A Culture of Kindness

Once you know how this applies to you, and you have done the work on yourself, you will have the ability to make positive impacts on your own happiness and the others around you. Some resources are listed in the Appendices to help you do your own self-evaluation.

5a.2   Energy

A culture of kindness is one that allows individuals to practice self compassion first so they can be equipped and strong to connect that to others, and it's one that is anchored in purpose. If we can come together in compassion and kindness, that to me is everything. It allows them to be vulnerable, to laugh and cry and be human.

Dani Savekar, CEO and Founder of GLAS group, visual synopsis and inspire kindness movement.

Your personal energy matters because it dictates how much you can deliver in a day. I would imagine that you already understand that. As a leader you may or may not already have arranged your daily routine to try and enhance your energy levels. This determines how you show up, tired and grumpy or attentive and energetic. So, how do you make sure that each day you are your best self but also how will you be kind to your team to allow them also to be their best selves? We often believe it has a lot to do with our possessions. Your home, your clothes, your family. However, the positivity that comes into your life starts on the inside, not even in a spiritual sense but in a very basic sense. Our routines and things we do can allow our energy levels to be enhanced or not. Unfortunately, not everyone is able to work out how best to support their own energy levels. They aren't aware of the things they could do or should consider. This is where the kind leader comes in, someone who is able to do more than just directing team members, but who understands the many ways in which humans find energy and want to share them. Energy is so often found in physical and mental wellbeing. I suggest that this section is an introduction and there are many books dedicated to the topics discussed. Even if it is not something for you, remember, this is about your team and what works for them.

Wellbeing

Our wellbeing is hugely important in every aspect of our lives. It affects our physical and mental health, but also our emotional day-to-day challenges. Wellbeing needs to take a holistic view of who we are and how we react to challenges, people and our environment. We should not rely solely on an organisation to pick up the slack on this, but to be sufficiently self-aware and have a clear idea of what is needed to achieve a positive sense of wellbeing. Wellbeing is as unique as a fingerprint, the challenge is just working out what yours looks like, and encouraging your staff to find out what their fingerprint looks like too. The top tip for this exercise is to try everything at least once.

Routines are great for people, but often the routine might be disrupted and be difficult to get back into. It is great to give examples of how to combat that, like using your mobile phone as an alarm to remind you. I have carved out a routine for myself and alarms tell me what I should be doing and when. It is a godsend! Little and often works better for me. Support yourself and your team by developing what works best for you and them.

Physical health

Doing regular exercise can feel like a huge burden anyway, but also a challenge that you need to build into an already busy day. We don't need to do hours of exercise every day, but we do need to get that heart rate going. So, if your team only run a mile each morning for example, they have squeezed a short burst of fitness into their day. How can you make it easy for them to build the things they love to do into their day?

There are many schools of thought about the best time to exercise, but I suggest people do what they feel is best for them to remain motivated. Running, hiit, dance classes, cycling, swimming, walking, yoga, pilates, gym, aerobics, tennis, or trampolining, whatever it is just don't make it a chore. Utilising time efficiently to ensure that your team are getting exercise at convenient times will ensure they are not adding extra stress needlessly to their day. It might be running for 15 minutes in their lunch break or first thing in the morning. Maybe it's that they exercise better with someone else rather than alone. You could organise half-hour lunchtime walks for the team. It's a great opportunity to chat too. This can also have positive effects on your relationships, motivations, and it releases good hormones.

If you are struggling with either your routine or how to work with particular team members on this then I recommend an hour-long coaching session with an ICF-accredited coach. The main thing is to find what works, create a routine and keep to it.

Mental health

It is impossible to avoid this topic nowadays, and consequently awareness of its importance has greatly increased. Research has demonstrated that our mental health has a direct effect on our physical health, (28) so we need to prioritise releasing tension as much as possible. Many of the actions laid out in the following chapters have the potential to improve mental health. However, this section provides overviews of some therapies you could suggest to your teams to build into their routines if they appeal. Of course, there are also many others available. Local meet ups and groups will allow you to try these out so, as I have said, try everything once. Another great way is to get your team to share what techniques they use, this helps develop more knowledge amongst the team as a whole.

Techniques to improve mental health might include acupuncture, Bowen technique, sound healing, massage, reiki and other energy healing methods, which many consider helpful in releasing stress.

A Culture of Kindness

Beyond the techniques listed above, more and more are being developed with scientific backing, including the few I mention below. You might want to consider finding a practitioner to try them out, or just reading more to gain an understanding of them. Even if you have never considered alternative therapies, you should remain up to date with the ways to support your own mental health and that of your team. It's not just about opening your own mind, but also about sharing that knowledge to others who may be able to benefit.

Tapping, or EFT – Emotional Freedom Technique
This is simple technique of tapping certain points on the upper part of your body which is considered to assist in releasing psychological and emotional blockages regarding certain aspects of your life, or a situation or challenge. EFT is believed to release stress and anxiety. For more information on this you can refer to the book *The Tapping Solution* by Nick Ortner among many others.

Mindfulness
Mindfulness is, in simple terms, bringing your awareness to the present. It contains elements of Buddhist traditions and is about bringing peace to yourself through meditation. The effect is understood to lower stress and anxiety, along with help with depression and drug addiction, among many other conditions. Mindfulness can be conducted through your own practices every day, however there are practitioners who can support this learning for you. Remember, try everything once. Rachel Sayles, teacher at Hayesfield Girls School, says in her podcast interview that bringing mindfulness into the curriculum has done wonders for the children, particularly around increasing their emotional intelligence.

CBT
Cognitive Behavioural Therapy is a form of talking therapy which focuses on our ability to challenge the cycle of thoughts, beliefs and behaviours that impact our feelings, actions and emotions. It is not the

traditional counselling talking approach you might imagine, but is based more on seeking out the problem point and discovering an action that will work to change the negative cycle. It is particularly useful if there are patterns of self destruction, reactions from other people or reactions to them that would appear to be holding back progress in the workplace for example. There are many supportive audio books to understand more about this technique, such as, *Cognitive Behavioural Therapy: Techniques for retraining your brain* by Professor Jason M Satterfield. (29)

NLP (Neuro Linguistic Programming)

I am a trained NLP master practitioner and coach. The technique is based on the idea of how language influences our minds. There has been considerable controversy over the techniques, mainly regarding whether it's based on an outdated idea of how the brain works. However, there are some very useful techniques, such as reframing, which means changing the way you see a situation. Or changing the language we use to explain things, such as if we tend to discuss things in an overly negative manner. The methodology is complicated but it is worth delving into for some of the key methods that you can build into your language to better inspire and motivate the people you interact with.

5a.3   Emotional Intelligence

It's paramount, you cannot make it if you don't have emotional intelligence in a leadership role. I see leaders with great intelligence but without the emotional intelligence you cannot improve. I see lots of smart people and their careers not prospering because of a lack of emotional intelligence. For me the crisis (Financial Crash) in the short term was not great for my career, but all the learning that I learnt about myself put me in a better place to grow professionally.

Guillermo Donadini – Chief Investment Officer – General Insurance (ex-Japan) at AIG

Emotional Intelligence is thought by many to be a key to not only success but also contentment. It is defined as the way to perceive and interpret emotions; or being able to name and regulate emotions to enhance your personal intellectual and emotional growth. Not raising your EQ (Emotional Quotient, the measurement of Emotional Intelligence) will not only affect your mental health but your physical health too. Relationships and prosperity will also be affected by the level of your EQ.

EQ is simply the other side of IQ, IQ being about the brain and EQ being about the emotions.

Increasing your EQ will not only benefit your life in general; but will support you in the challenges you face each day. EQ sets a strong foundation for dealing with the current very transient culture in which we live. It helps with the following:

- Enables you to make better decisions
- Increases your ability to communicate well, through a calmer and clearer mind
- Supports you better in coping with the daily struggles of life

- Neutralises conflicts with ease
- Your empathy is increased and therefore making new friends is made easier

There are generally four key skills around Emotional Intelligence to be aware of when you want to increase your EQ.

Self awareness - This is where you are able to name and recognise your emotions including the effect that they have on your physical being.

Self-management - This is being able to control emotions so that they don't take control of your actions. At moments where you are unable to recognise an emotion, it will take hold of your being. Good self-management is not holding back emotions but recognising them so that you are able to manage them.

Social awareness – This is being able to understand what people around you are feeling as well as their concerns and needs. It is hugely beneficial to growing relationships but also allows you to read situations and manage those moments in a positive way, even when they might not be that pleasant.

Relationship management - In many ways once you have the above this fourth skills falls into place on its own. Having the ability to build and maintain strong relationships is key to judging situations and the actions you take. At this stage you can inspire others and generally be a great team player.

I am sure you will agree EQ is pretty important and the great news is we can raise it easily.

First, recognise your negative emotions. 'Recognise, accept and then release' is a great motto. It is a simple practice, but needs you to own the emotion, which is sometimes terrifying to start with but actually with very little practice becomes the best tool you will ever use. There are many techniques on how to do this, but for now, start by looking at what caused the negative emotion. We are often afraid to tackle the issue. But time spent noticing your emotions is hugely important so that you are then able to change the state. Of course, this is only a summary, and there are hundreds of ways to change state, it's what works for you as I have suggested in the previous chapter on mental health.

Using distraction techniques - This is great once you have accepted and noticed the emotion. Sometimes you just need a distraction. To do something, be around someone that helps you to move out of the negative state. Find your distraction.

Positive affirmations - This means feeding your brain with positive affirmations about yourself. If you're at a loss, you could try 'You tube' will supply you with loads of inspiration for this too. Make your own list of positive affirmations when you feel good, or ask your friends and family to tell you good things about yourself, then write them all down. Then when negative emotions come upon you, read out your own affirmations and remind yourself of the truth.

Listening to stories - This might include watching TED talks and other stories that invoke feelings. Being able to empathise is hugely important in raising EQ.

Mindfulness and mediation - If you are able to make these a part of your life not only will your EQ increase, but they support so many other aspects of life, such as increasing happiness and mental clarity.

Make down time happen – No one wins if you work 16-hour days, so schedule some down time and really ensure that you close yourself to work to give yourself hobbies that you enjoy.

We are aware that we must do physical exercise to stay fit and healthy, however for the rest of the book I want you to consider that your mind also needs that work out. You are conscious of what you feed your body, not too much sugar or fat, for example. It is the same for your brain. Don't let it be fed with negativity.

We will now look at each of the four areas in more detail. Consider these the walls to your house.

5a.4   Self-Awareness

While all the areas are equally important, if you don't enhance your self-awareness you are less likely to be able to enhance the other three areas that make up Emotional Intelligence (self-management, social awareness and relationship management). Being aware of yourself, the effect you have on others and who you are is important in not only your work but also how and when you have relationships and friendships in any form. If you aren't able to identify who you are, you cannot fully understand the effect you have on others, nor why relationships may fail.

5a.5   Understand your emotions

Understanding your emotions would appear to be the simplest thing in the world, particularly when you read it as an instruction such as, 'Understand your emotions', simple. Our brains say, 'yep I do that, I know when I am angry, sad, happy. I've got that covered'.

If I take you back just a moment, how often do you use the word, 'powerless' or 'inferior' or 'disappointed' to describe your sadness? They are all sadness but so often we will generalise with our emotions. However, that is like sticking to reading picture books even though we have learnt to read. Having a better understanding and acceptance of our emotions often comes in the form of emotional vocabulary. I have in Appendix 8.4 given you a couple of examples developed from Robert Plutchik's Wheel of Emotions.

Each human can experience 34,000 emotions, however we tend to stick to just 8 average emotions. So being able to better define this allows us to grow our emotional intelligence for self-awareness. If we understand our emotions, we have a far greater chance of having control over our reactions.

ACTION

A top tip for you and/or your teams is that everyone has the wheel of emotions in their diary, on the fridge or pinboard. Make it something that is well looked at and used day to day. Individuals should use it to refer to daily at a set time each day to look at what emotions they have felt that day. Having a set time may seem too prescriptive, however if you don't do that we get busy with other things and don't do the training our brain needs. It's a little like if you go to a gym class, you always schedule a set time. You could use an alarm on your phone or diarising, whatever works for your time management. Of course, it is also excellent to be used when an emotional situation occurs as this takes some of the heat out of the moment. However, by doing it daily, it is like testing your emotional fitness.

A Culture of Kindness

5a.6   Accept your feelings

We are taught wrongly don't cry its weak, it's one of the most annoying sentences someone can say, because it's a massively strong emotion in you and it's a release, so you wouldn't tell someone not to laugh.

Ricky Manetta, Founder of MMA Krav Maga and a head coordinator with the UFC

This is like the tough workout so many people struggle with at the gym, probably the equivalent of a spinning class. We know humans struggle with feelings because there are so many ways to numb the pain that feelings can often give us.

To briefly define emotions and feelings, Six Seconds, the organisation that researches emotional intelligence, describes it best:

Emotions are chemicals released in response to our interpretation of a specific trigger. It takes our brains about 1/4 second to identify the trigger, and about another 1/4 second to produce the chemicals. By the way, emotion chemicals are released throughout our bodies, not just in our brains, and they form a kind of feedback loop between our brains & bodies. They last for about six seconds. (Hence their name)

Feelings happen as we begin to integrate the emotion, to think about it, to "let it soak in." In English, we use the word "feel" for both physical and emotional sensation — we can say we physically feel cold, but we can also emotionally feel cold. This is a clue to the meaning of "feeling," it's something we sense. Feelings become more "cognitively saturated" as the emotion chemicals are processed in our brains & bodies. They are often fuelled by a mix of emotions, and last longer than emotions.

Moods are more generalised. They're not tied to a specific incident, but a collection of inputs. Mood is heavily influenced by several factors: the environment (weather, lighting, people around us), physiology (what we've been eating, how we've been exercising, how healthy we are), and finally our mental state (where we're focusing attention and our current emotions). Moods can last minutes, hours, probably even days. (30)

In summary, simply think of the emotions as the short version and feelings as the longer version. However, it's hard to accept them either way, and most of us struggle with riding those waves and being ok with that without drowning. We talk about negative and positive, but to really accept them we have to try as hard as we can to eliminate that conditioning. Having any sort of feeling is neither good nor bad, it just is what it is. Very much as mindfulness teaches us, allowing emotions and feelings to pass through without wishing them away or wanting them more, we start to accept them. The consequence of not accepting feelings is that we simply become numb, hiding and blocking the emotions and feelings instead, using alcohol and such to do this. All emotions and feelings are there because our brains react to our circumstances, they are there to keep us safe and out of danger. However sometimes in fact we are not in danger but our brain believes we could be, for example when some people are more nervous taking a plane ride than someone else. Acceptance at this point is the key to allowing the emotions and feelings to pass through and not get stuck or numbing that feeling through alcohol or other addictions to food, drugs or sex.

ACTION

Mindfulness is considered to be a meditation technique and some believe that people who meditate are healthier, happier and more successful than those who don't. Instilling it into the workplace would then make perfect sense. Of course, you can't force people to take part, but there are many ways in which you can make this more accessible. For example, by setting up group mindfulness in the workplace before and/or at the end of the working day. Include leaflets in the induction process that explains its benefits, or provide access to an audio or written book on mindfulness.

You will find a mindfulness-based treatment program by Fleming and Kocovski (2007) aimed at reducing social anxiety on the (Act on Social Anxiety website. (31) This may particularly benefit younger members of your team. You will find it useful in any setting, but those that find social interaction challenging will benefit most because their exposure has been limited in this regard.

Ideally your organisation could invite a practitioner to deliver mindfulness each week with employees, but if this is not practical then you can use the techniques to start something within your office, or alternatively empower one of your staff to undergo training and set up their own course of mindfulness in return. Testing the results on how your staff feel will be invaluable.

5a.7   What affects you and why

When we know what has an effect on us, and why, we start to understand how to get more positive results from our actions. We also feel we have more control over our reactions.

Emotions can be triggered, meaning that an event or stimulus reminds us of previous experiences. This is because human brains are efficient and we tend to form neural pathways, and therefore follow patterns. Patterns can be great because it means in many ways we can predict and control those emotions.

Emotional triggers have effects on your physical body, such as increased heartrate, sweaty palms, or that odd sensation of weakness in your legs or when you feel heat run through your body. We all have our individual reactions so this is a great way to understand how your emotions affect you. If you can do this you can work back to discover what that trigger was. From a business point of view, encouraging your staff to do this work for themselves makes for a more harmonious environment.

For example, –let's say someone is triggered by the use of negative words such as can't, don't etc, and it causes them to be angry and frustrated. If they have identified that about themselves they are able to recognise a need to change the conversation when they encounter a person who uses this kind of language. This idea of looking for our triggers can be utilised in many ways, but the important point here is the delving into the reasons for each reaction which allows us to become more self aware. In turn we will approach situations and people more generously and kindly.

ACTION

When we encounter an emotion we need to take a minute to think through our physical reactions, as this will bring some awareness of the feeling and also acceptance. Encourage staff as well as yourself at this point to keep a diary for this to evaluate each day, noting the emotion they felt and the physical reaction, along with whether they understand the trigger. The idea is they will then be able to evaluate this. To have self-awareness you need data, which you look at to establish patterns and then build knowledge. Knowledge, as the saying goes, is power. With knowledge you can control your emotions in situations to ensure your relationships are healthy and of course, kind.

I have designed a diary sheet for you to use and suggest that this is completed for 30 days as shown in Appendix 8.6. You can copy this and make your own booklets for ongoing analysis.

5a.8 Your personality

We think we know ourselves and my guess without scientific research is that you do on a fundamental level. However, we are always learning about ourselves, and the impacts things have had on us. At the Way with Words festival in 2019, Robin Ince, the comedian, spoke about his life and how, when he had been very little, he had been in a car accident that had left his mother with permanent damage. He described how it is only after a long period of time that you can actually look back and see the velocity, impact and the reactions to life challenges that you have had, do you really ever know their effects?

Our personalities are important as they allow people to connect with us or not as the case may be. We are not, as they say, everyone's cup of tea because we are all unique. Personality is made up of not only innate traits but those that develop over time and with experience. Our personalities and traits lead our behaviour, and that is why it's so important to understand someone's personality; to understand why they behave in a certain way. Psychologists have theorised how personality forms, and we have touched earlier on Lawrence Kohlberg's theory because he bases his idea on morals. In this book too, morals are emphasised.

So, can you change your personality? Freud believed your personality is set from the age of five as discussed in his theory Id, Ego and Super Ego. (32) However, what happens if we do all this work on ourselves and realise that we just don't really like our personality all that much? What if it just isn't helping in developing relationships?

The debate over nature and nurture has raged for years. Today most would agree that the answer lies in a mixture of the two.

Not only that, but the constant interaction between genetics and the environment can help shape how personality comes across. For example, you might be predisposed to being kind and friendly, but working in a high-stress environment might lead you to be more short-tempered and uptight than you might be in a different setting.

Studies (33) demonstrate that upbringing and even culture also interact with the part of personality that is made up by genetics to shape who we are.

Psychologist Carole Dweck (34) suggests that personality change is in fact possible. There may be core traits that are consistent, but Dweck believes that our in-between qualities are the most important factor in who we are day to day, and those can be influenced.

So, what are these 'in-between' parts of personality?
Beliefs and belief systems, Dweck proposes, play a vital role in shaping personality beyond the level of the broad traits. While changing certain aspects of your personality might be challenging, you can realistically tackle changing some of the underlying beliefs that shape and control how your personality is expressed.

Other theorists have suggested that factors such as goals and coping strategies play a primary role in determining personality. For example, while you might have more of a Type A personality, (35) you can learn new coping skills and stress management techniques that help you become a more relaxed person.

Why focus on beliefs? Our beliefs shape so much of our lives, and who we are, how we see ourselves, how we manage day to day, how we deal with life's challenges, and how we forge connections with other people. If we can create even slight change in our beliefs, it can affect our behaviours and in time our personality.

Take, for example, beliefs about yourself, if you believe your intelligence is fixed, then you are not likely to take steps to deepen your thinking. If, however, you view such characteristics as changeable, you are likely to make a greater effort to challenge yourself and broaden your mind.

Interestingly, Dweck's own research has demonstrated that how children are praised can have an impact on their self-beliefs. Those who are praised for their intelligence tend to hold fixed-theory beliefs about their own personal attributes. These children view their intelligence as an unchangeable trait; you either have it or you don't. Children who are praised for their efforts, on the other hand, typically view their intelligence as something they can improve. These children, Dweck has found, tend to persist in the face of difficulty and are more eager to learn. (36)

Changing from an introvert to an extrovert might appear very difficult, however positive psychologist Christopher Peterson realised early on that his introverted personality might have a detrimental impact on his career as an academic. To overcome this, he decided to start acting extroverted in situations that called for it, for example when he had to deliver a lecture or presentation. Eventually, these behaviours simply become second nature. While he suggested that he was still an introvert, he learned how to become extroverted when he needed to be.

Here are a couple of other things that experts suggest.

Focus on changing your habits. Psychologists have found that people who exhibit positive personality traits (such as kindness and honesty) develop habitual responses that become engrained into their personality. Of course, forming a new habit or breaking an old one is never easy. With enough practice though they can become second nature. So those organisational morals will instill positive change and therefore consistency.

A Culture of Kindness

Change your self-beliefs. If you believe you cannot change, then you will not change. If you are trying to become more outgoing, but you believe that your introversion is a fixed, permanent, and unchangeable trait, then you will simply never try to become more sociable. If you say you can't you probably won't.

Focus on the process. Dweck's research has consistently shown that praising actions rather than the person had better outcomes for positive change. Instead of thinking 'I'm so intelligent', or 'I'm so clever', replace such phrases with 'I worked really hard' or 'I found a good way of solving that problem.' This is all about shifting to a growth, rather than fixed, mindset. You may find that it is easier to experience real change and growth that way.

ACTION

This one is simple. Complete a personality profiling test. I have placed several in Appendix 8.2 to use. If you are a leader, get your team to complete them and then book a time to talk about them in an informal one-to-one setting. This is a great way to build bonds with your team but also to better understand the person so you can lead them with kindness first and foremost on the basis of who they are. Accepting people for who they are is key to building trust and strength in your teams. However, there may be parts of the personality profiling that a person identifies for improvement and this can be done with support. You can use this information to start to predict what some of the organisational morals you have adopted are likely to have on this person. Will it cause change, or will it enhance some already existing personality traits? Either way, it will affect the person and you should be mindful of that.

A Culture of Kindness

5a.9   Your values

Values are everything. If you don't know your core values and have not done the work to define them, we are going to that now. If you have, then let's do it again. You and the people around you will be better informed and happier with this knowledge. Allow me to give you a scenario to evidence why values matter at work.

Nick and Sam work opposite each other in an office nine-to-five, Monday to Friday. They do exactly the same job, but Nick is responsible for the North of England and Sam is responsible for the South. Their roles are to organise different contractors who visit people's homes to carry out maintenance works. It requires planning skills, and to have a proactive approach to limiting reactionary works. Many of the tasks require a methodical approach. Routine is key.

Nick is a family man, he enjoys his time at home after work. He wishes he could be home earlier. However, he really enjoys his work, he loves the fact he can cycle to work, leaving his home at exactly 8.40am after walking his children to school. Nick's values are family, security and reliability.

Sam is a single man, he is a climber in his spare time, and loves the outdoors more than anything else. He plays guitar and enjoys festivals and music events. He is a free spirit. His values are freedom, spirituality and humour.

Nick is very happy within his role, however Sam is not. This is because the role and the tasks within the role do not match the values of the human. We are all different.

We must stop trying to squeeze the square peg into the round hole. We keep trying to value people on what they can deliver rather than who they are and how they feel about the work. When we consider who they are first and foremost, what they deliver will be more significant than we or even they thought possible.

ACTION

We are going to run through the quickest and easiest way to establish your core values. There are more complex methods that will allow you to discover a higher self-awareness, but for now this will work for you personally and for your team.

First go through your personality profile and pick out all the values that show up. These can be things like commitment, honesty, insightfulness, integrity and so on.

Once you have done that, use the list of values in Appendix 7 to add those that you think apply to you. Please be careful not to include at this point values you want to have but maybe don't yet possess.

You could have at this point about 30 values. Write them each onto post-it notes or small pieces of paper. Once you have done this, go through and start to group them by similarity. You will probably have a few groups of values at this point, but from each group there will be one that sticks out more than any other. You are trying to narrow down the groups to a set of core values. Core values usually number between three and five.

For example, you may end up with a group including kind, altruistic, compassionate, empathetic and considered. I might choose altruistic if it feels most true for me, while someone else may have the same list but for them, empathetic might stand out more.

Each group of values that you have at this point should now have one core value. Pull them out and put them together.

Look at them again, decide whether there are any that repeat themselves, or could be narrowed down further. Aim to produce a list of between three and five values as I have previous said.

For the rest of the week it is worth considering moments in your life that you have felt uncomfortable or unhappy and then consider if you had been living at that time in your life by values other than those you have highlighted.

I'll leave that to you.

5a.10   Who are you?

Who are you? We don't often ask that. When we ask others about themselves we ask, what do you do? What's your name? Where do you live. But when we meet someone we rarely say, who are you? We often don't even consider asking ourselves this question and that, I believe, is such a terrible shame. Who you are can be evaluated in the actions you are taking through the book but also based on the roles you play in life to others and what that means to you.

Understanding your various roles has several benefits. First it obviously brings about higher self-awareness almost instantly. In the long term it allows you to analyse the differences in the roles and how to move from one role to the other. Also, why sometimes there is discomfort as you switch from one role to another. Being aware of this can make such a difference in how you handle those challenges.

ACTION

In appendix 5 you will find a sheet that you can use to consider the roles you play to others and how you feel about that. For example: *I am a mother. I am required to be responsible, I need to stay calm in the madness of life with my two boys. I am required to listen and be totally present with my boys.* You get the idea.

And so it goes on, including your job roles, friendships, club memberships. Your roles will often be very different and demand you consider different aspects of yourself, so use the information to your advantage.   You'll find examples at the top of the sheet for your reference.

5a.11   Evaluate your emotions

I have touched on this but will mention it again. The time after strong emotional episodes is a good opportunity to evaluate them. Spend some time considering where those feelings came from and why. I am not speaking about just the emotions that we avoid, but also those we seek out. All our feelings are available to evaluate for our future. It helps to see emotions as data to allow us to grow and increase our self-awareness. Start by taking advantage of the emotional diary in Appendix 8.6 for 30 days.

Having greater self-awareness is the foundation of how we continue to strive but also interact with people kindly. We are unkind in our uncertainty of not only situations but also of ourselves. We make the world better by first understanding ourselves.

A Culture of Kindness

5b   Self management

Self management is the focus on how we manage and control ourselves and our emotions. It includes how we manage our impulses.

5b.1   Breathe (Stress management)

Manage your breath. That's right, breathe! Have you ever found yourself in a stressful situation and discovered that you were holding your breath? Mindfulness all begins with pausing, taking a deep breath and exhaling fully. Give it a try. Breathe in for four counts and breathe out for six counts, repeat five times.

Managing your breath is a simple way to see more clearly how you can activate other areas of self-management. In your teams encourage it as a coping mechanism for the day-to-day stresses that work brings. There are so many unique ways in which you can incorporate this into your business. For example, use technology. If we can monitor our heart rate using watches, we can no doubt set reminders to remind ourselves to take a breath.

The technical reason for why breath works so well can be summarised as, when we have something that causes us stress, it is similar to the fear humans experienced when they were chased by those sabre tooth tigers that we discussed earlier. The threats we experience today are mostly not on that level, but the brain still works the same way and therefore releases the same hormones that provoke us to hold our breath, clench our jaws and take on the physical attributes that we would if we saw the sabre tooth tiger.

When we become aware of this as described in Chapter 5a.4 on self-awareness, we start to be able to make a change.

ACTION

For you personally or your team, set up a way to remind people to breathe through their challenges. It could be post-it notes on the computer, screensavers, posters, writing words on the office wall or even technical solutions. I'd love to see what you have chosen, you can share them on twitter by tagging @SummersNahla being sure to #breathchallenge #cultureofkindness.

5b.2   Use self-awareness

By completing all the things you did in Chapter 5a.9 you will have started to make a list of what defines you. I hope that you have started to recognise your strengths. If you haven't, take a moment now to list them (There is a place in the back of the book for this). Your strengths are those things that people draw upon for you, for example, maybe you listen well. Maybe you are good at managing your time or have tenacity. There are thousands of strengths that you probably have and listing them out is important. Some of you may feel uncomfortable listing them if it feels like bragging, but understanding our strengths is important for many reasons, including:

- We can gain a higher self-awareness.
- We can focus energy in the right place to grow.
- We are able to give better to people around us.

Consideration should also be given to our weaknesses (I prefer to call these weak points. They are not failings, they are things that we recognise we don't do so well.) As with anything in life, we can improve in everything if we choose to. For example, if you find that you have a short concentration span you may consider looking at your health and the foods you eat, you may look at a morning routine that works on part of the brain that will improve your concentration. It might even become a strength in time. Some benefits of working on our weaker points are:

- We gain a higher self-awareness from understanding our weak points.
- It gives us something to consider and work on to improve overall wellbeing.
- We are better able to understand how we affect others around us.

Using the knowledge of not only our strengths and weaknesses but also emotional triggers, belief systems, values and default cultural position among many others, you can start to investigate. You can then use this knowledge to manage yourself.

So, what does managing yourself in those trickier situations look like? You must have been in a position in the past where you have 'seen red' and been so mad you can't control your reactions. Maybe you've felt overwhelmingly needy or sad over a situation? By doing the work on self we are better able to manage those reactions because we better understand where they come from. Simple really, but it is the key to so much; an understanding of self.

ACTION

Complete the Strengths and Weaknesses list in Appendix 8.5. You can ask friends and family to help. It's probably best not to ask those who find it hard to be objective, or not to be judgmental. You are looking for useful information on how others see you that you can take forward. If you can, ask five people. You will start to see the patterns.

A Culture of Kindness

5b.3 Not everyone is you

The topic of judgement takes us smoothly onto, 'not everyone is you'. As a leader, a wife, a brother, whatever your roles are in life, it is so easy to expect those we work with or know well to behave similarly and have a similar ethic. We seek out people who are like us and when they do something that is not what we would do we become very upset. Therefore, this is a really important phrase that I strongly advise you take on board as a daily mantra, '**Not everyone is the same**'. We start to accept the nuances a little more easily when we continually remind ourselves of this very important fact. Everyone has different life experiences, and personalities vary.

There is no specific action you can do to fix this human conditioning without simply being more self-aware. This will allow you to manage situations better. You will more likely find a tolerance that helps manage your feelings toward a person with more acceptance.

5b.4 Time management

Time management is all about organising yourself and its effects are huge. Let's look first at that feeling of not managing your time. Everything is in disarray, you don't get that great feeling of achieving things where you have that wonderful release of dopamine into your body. The effects of feeling right compared with disorganised chaos are astonishing.

Having a good time-management plan will mean that you and the people around you will achieve more in the time you have because you are organised. If one person in a group is disorganised it will affect the people around them in many ways. Encouraging everyone into a working environment to be organised will help them develop their own ways to manage time effectively. The effect is that individuals and groups will become calmer, have less stress and achieve more, not just for the company but for themselves.

Allow people to decide on their system, there are many different ways in which they might manage their time and this is a personal choice that each individual must work through. Make time to coach, support and discuss the systems they choose. If you are not organised you are not being kind to your team or even yourself as you will increase stress levels for yourself and others.

ACTION

There are entire books dedicated to this topic, so I am going to keep this part simple. If you are a leader I recommend doing a time management training day for your team.

Use a diary – Look around and work out how you are going to use it to plan and record things and your to-do list.

Dream – Dreaming and imagining all the things you would like to achieve is important. Equally important is finding a way to achieve them. Make a list of all your dreams, the life list. There is a blank page on Appendix 8 for this.

For each of your dreams there will be a lot of tiny actions that you need to take to get you to your dream. So, for example, if you plan to cycle around the world, you will need to get a bike, you will need to dedicate time to train. You will start to build a list of all the tiny actions to achieve your main goal. When you look to diarise those tiny actions, the magic really happens. I suggest you use the GROW online workshop to virtually work through how to do this and make it less daunting.

A Culture of Kindness

5b.5   Motivation

What is our motivation? Where do we get motivation from? How do we motivate others around us? Motivation is so key to how we manage ourselves and also allows us to achieve the goals and tasks we set ourselves each day. So, what can we do to gain more?

Vanderbilt University conducted a study where scientists mapped the brains of both go-getters and slackers. (37) The study showed that those who were *willing to work hard for rewards had higher dopamine levels. The dopamine was in the striatum and PFC, which are both linked to motivation and reward.* With slackers, however, dopamine was only found in the parts of the brain associated with emotion and risk perception.

Our motivation levels are related to how difficult we perceive a task to be, and the perceived rewards that come from completing that task. *This means that when there are low rewards, the motivation to power through a task is likely to be lower. If the perceived difficulty of a task suddenly increases during a period of low motivation, our motivation level will then drop even further.* This will eventually lead to *a downward spiral in motivational level unless we do something to override this.*

The exciting thing about developing motivation is that it can come quite naturally once you or your team have worked on self-awareness. When we understand what a person's needs are, we can motivate with ease.

This can also slot very nicely into time management. For example, setting achievable goals and being able to easily tick items off the list is a great motivator. To do this you would want to break down the big task into smaller tasks. So if for example you need to provide a report and that might feel monotonous and not something you might relish, the idea is to break it into smaller tasks that you then add to your diary to do on particular days and times as I have mentioned before. This allows you to tackle the tasks in a more manageable way and also get the benefit of ticking items off. This not only releases dopamine, but also the more you tick off, the more motivated you become. You may already do this, and you may think of it as unimportant, however not everyone has this knowledge so it's important to share this with your team and give them guidance on how they can help themselves.

When I was younger, I had a mentor who told me that the secret to everything in life is the ability to train your brain, and in so many aspects of life he was correct. Our brains react, as previously discussed, in a very primitive way. It has the fight or flight response, which can have a major effect on motivation. So, for example when we say, 'I **am** bored with this' we make it about us, it's personal as though it is actually our very being. It's very hard to shift that mindset. However, if you were to say in your conversation with yourself, 'I **feel** bored with this', you can understand it is a moment in time, that by breaking down the tasks that boredom is likely to pass much more easily.

Motivating your team can be enhanced as follows:
Listening to people (See Chapter 5c.1)
Integrity, being honest and sticking by your word. Owning mistakes.
Reduce stress (See Chapter 5b.1)
Know who needs you (See Chapter 5d.8)
Giving feedback – This is not covered elsewhere so let's look at it here.

Feedback is usually seen as the place to talk to someone about the things that they aren't doing well. However, as Brené Brown says in her TED talk, (38) we get told 30 things that we are doing great, and the one thing we aren't doing well is the thing that we focus on and which gets stuck in our heads. Feedback should evolve from the person, not be told to them. If someone in your team is growing their self-awareness on a daily basis as you would be encouraging by using this book and your own resources, you would expect them to also be able to start to look at what they might want to improve on.

Feedback that is short term and immediate can also come from the person if you use the standard coaching method of questioning.
- How do you think that went?
- What would you do if you were to do it again?
- What parts do you think met the client's needs the most?
- What do you think you might adapt if you were to present again?

Use questions that open the person's mind rather than something that just becomes criticism.

Please allow me to digress a minute. In all my years in a corporate setting in various countries around the world, I have come to discover that criticism is the easiest thing to dish out but the hardest to produce anything good from. However, it's the way many people provide feedback. 'I don't like...', 'That won't work...', 'Can we not have ...', 'That's not what they asked for....'. The common theme is the negativity in each line and also how quickly the comments are delivered. 'We are in a hurry in life and really don't have time for a Q and A', many people will say. However, the long-term effect of taking the extra five minutes to ask a different question will mean the results are growth, motivation and improved staff wellbeing.

So, let's turn some of these criticism into motivators.

CRITICISM	MOTIVATOR
I don't like that ...	That's interesting, what made you decide to do it like that ...?
That won't work ...	Interesting, what makes you believe that will work as the best option...?

Can we not have...	I like this idea. Have you considered ...?
That is not what they asked for...	What were your thoughts in how this will match what they asked for?

With the first questions, there is very little room for any movement or growth in the conversation. However, when we slow it down, draw out the questions with positivity, you can see that there are follow-on questions which allow people to contribute, which do not feel like a put-down, but instead the person feels developed and shaped to consider all the factors. They may have considered all the factors and have simply got a better idea than you, the leader. As Steve Jobs said, always hire people smarter than you. If that's the case, why would you want to criticise rather than look to simply understand their mindset around a task?

There is also the method I like for when a group is becoming particularly critical and unhelpful. Encourage the group to only add to the project. No one is allowed to remove or say they don't like. You can only add. From that the leader will then in a structured way bring together all the ideas. This also means everyone is invested so they want to it work.

In the beautiful classic, *The Prophet*, Kahlil Gibran shares the concept that work is simply something we do to contribute to society, to make the world go around and for the survival of all people. (39) When we understand that concept it is easier to find work less of a chore. We are all motivated by certain things as David Rock's SCARF (40) model illustrates. The way the brain responds to perceived threats and rewards relates to a person's relative importance to others, so provide feedback that aids the recipient's status. Avoid feedback that threatens it as I have already discussed. The brain's response to threats and rewards:

- is about being able to predict the future. Staff knowing what they are working towards needs to be clear. Being secretive is not motivating. See Chapter 6.2 on trust.
- provides a sense of control over events for your team. Micromanaging only demotivates. But 'certainty' must have happened first.
- is the sense of connection and safety with others (the brain perceives a friend versus a foe). Fostering a culture of teamwork and connectivity to increase relatedness.
- is the perception of being treated justly. Treat your team with dignity and respect. Also make sure that they are compensated fairly and have job security.

In summary, without your team feeling motivated productivity goes down. While we all have to attempt to motivate ourselves, you as leader has an effect on the motivation of the people around you, be mindful of that.

A Culture of Kindness

5b.6   Your health

We all talk about it, we all know it's important, but often focus on the way we look rather than genuine health. The diet industry is a multi-billion pound business because it markets to our weaknesses about how we look. However, our health is not so much about how we look as about how we feel. How we feel and function is by far the most important thing about health. Self management comes into play here. What actions do we undertake to feel better and ultimately be healthy?

Let's look at addictions first and foremost. Addictions come in many forms, to smoking, alcohol, drugs, gambling, sex, and the one less discussed, which is to food and sugar. Sugar activates the same reward system, dopamine, as motivation, but also cocaine and nicotine. There is still some scientific debate on this, but we can't disagree that many use sugar as a boost when we lack energy, and that we experience lows afterwards. This is not conducive to having strong self management.

The recent debate about the gut microbiome asks whether all our health issues originate in the gut, and whether addressing this by taking better care of our digestive system, will resolve many other health issues. I will share with you a personal story to illustrate.

In 2018 it took me two months to cycle across America, but by month one I was clearly unwell. My stomach was uncomfortable with some pretty unpleasant side effects. I had at the time just thought it was something I must have eaten, but this went on for months. When I got back to the UK, I had lost half a stone that I could not afford to lose and when I went to the doctor I was swiftly tested for bowel cancer. Thankfully I did not have cancer, and the testing process actually helped my systems to normalise. I knew things weren't quite right but was muddling on. I had always enjoyed an afternoon sleep if circumstances allowed, and it had been a tradition for my grandfather and me to snooze in front of the Saturday afternoon crime drama on ITV3. My skin, poor sleep and emotional wellbeing had been a concern but nothing I couldn't manage through good skin treatment, reading books at night and self-awareness techniques.

At that point I discovered Synergy. There are many companies which now specialise in this, however for me Synergy is what I know so I use them as an example (They are not paying me for this incidentally it is simply that I can't talk about any other experience!)

Before I went on my 500-mile walk the year after the cycle ride I said that when I returned I would do the Synergy 21-day reset program. This is designed to reset the gut to health, and has larger consequences for your health generally. After the program, the difference in me was quite astonishing. I discovered that I had obviously been affected by the many antibiotics I had had to take over the years for several bouts of pleurisy and other diseases, but it also emerged that I had a serious addiction to sugar that affected my ability to manage myself. Microbiome is a whole topic in itself, however what is indisputable is that, when you address your health and really purify everything you put into your body, that you make not only an impact on physical health and quite rapidly in some cases also, and this is the one I love, on your mental health. Maybe the rise in processed foods and meals along with the rise in stress and anxiety is no coincidence.

ACTION

Promote healthier eating. Ask people to consider their food intake by informing them of the benefits of balancing the microbiome. You can also provide healthy snacks for people in an office environment. Working towards optimal health will allow you to manage yourself better. (I have placed in Appendix a reference for Synergy).

5b.7   Confidence

Confidence! Oh, that elusive daily struggle. We are endlessly fascinated by other people's seeming over- or under-supply of confidence. Really it is about having self-belief and self-esteem. The good news is that this will happen naturally for you and your teams by following the actions within the book. So, for example having a better grip on time management will naturally cause you to feel more confident. By understanding yourself you will of course naturally start to feel more confident. Feeling better in your health and lowering your stress levels will also have those positive effects. Maslow's hierarchy of needs (41) is a wonderful tool to determine whether your team have everything they need to create a strong sense of self actualisation.

For those who are unfamiliar with Maslow's hierarchy, note the tiered system in the diagram. Maslow said that an individual needed to gain the bottom of the triangle to build up to the peak and the point of self actualisation. He also clarified later that a person did not need to gain complete perfection in an area, but to have the basics of each section, which would be the security and contentment of each area. This is so important as, through our work and in building a culture of kindness, we can have such a strong influence on allowing those around us to create a strong sense of self.

Self confidence, which I would suggest is something close to self actualisation, is what we admire and respect in people who seem to have the right levels of confidence. They usually have a positive attitude towards themselves and others.

Self confidence means having a positive and balanced attitude. When obstacles occur, a person with a confident attitude continues to work to overcome the challenges, whereas someone lacking self confidence is unlikely to persevere and might not even have a go at starting something. They are maybe paralysed by fear and this can occur if too much criticism takes place at some point in their lives. Overcoming barriers and giving ourselves and others praise for what has been achieved is important to building confidence. Lord Mark Price in his book talks about six stages of fairness at work, and one of those is based on the idea of praise. It means saying thank you and being grateful. As previously discussed, Sally Waterston says that companies should realise that they must be grateful that people come to work for them, not the other way around. This is very much based on Maslow's idea of building esteem.

As mentioned, there is a fine line between over confidence which can be off-putting, and low confidence which affects our ability to achieve things. Overconfidence is destructive to teams and in turn to you as an individual.

However, a lack of confidence manifests in several ways. Signs of a confidence problem include difficulty admitting mistakes, an unwillingness to apologise, bragging, or a pushiness that borders on bullying. While bragging could appear to be confidence on the surface, people who are truly confident have no need to brag; those who do are often trying to convince themselves of their own worth. Also, when we are so worried about looking incompetent in the eyes of others that we can't admit our own shortcomings, we are not likely to take advantage of coaching and advice from peers and potential mentors. But if we are to develop high EQ and become successful, this is exactly what we must do!

We judge confidence by whether or not someone is able to look us in the eye, by whether they speak up at challenging times, by body language, the way they walk and carry themselves, and by how much initiative and determination they display.

Finding the right level of confidence is important as not only a leader but also as a team player. If you aren't confident in your message and who you are, the people around you will also not be confident in your leadership and in working with you.

So how do we really know if we are too confident if we are already have that as a personality trait? It takes some healthy self-awareness to draw it out. If you think you could be squashing the people around you with your overconfidence, there are a few things you can try to resolve this.

If we are overconfident, people will accuse us of being pushy. We seldom apologise or admit we are wrong. We might even pride ourselves in this, but others don't like this behaviour. In fact, the confidence of the know-it-all is a barrier to good communication and to developing positive relationships within a group. Most people resent know-it-alls and they are unwilling to give these bossy, overconfident people what they want.

People with a genuine belief in themselves do not have trouble admitting they are wrong and apologising for mistakes. We all make mistakes, so knowing that is a sign of self-awareness and confidence that you know yourself. People who are honest and speak with a justified sense of confidence will get people onside with them. When we let go of the need to have all the answers and learn to be a little more vulnerable, then can we move from the know-it-all to a person of true self confidence and therefore gain respect rather than lose it.

Genuine confidence helps us balance our needs with those of other people, and this will lead to more success in relationship management (see Chapter 5d).

The important part of this is not allowing ego on either end of the scale to take over your interactions with others. This management of self will allow you to grow, admit mistakes and have a healthy, thriving environment and impact on others.

ACTION

A few things contribute to increasing in confidence and gaining a better understanding of self. Some of those you are already doing.

Positive affirmations – (see Chapter 5a.3)

Make an effort on yourself – Whatever that looks like. It could be the way you hold yourself, your clothes, to ensure you smile more in the day, read something to help your knowledge. Making an effort on yourself will in turn support your confidence.

A Culture of Kindness

Opportunities - Look for chances to present at work or clubs where you can present and be part of something.

Pre-plan scenarios – There will be situations where you can work through conversations in your mind to give you more confidence about a situations. For example, if you are about to go into a meeting where you need to present a piece of work, start to imagine and predict all the questions that might be asked so you can pre-plan your responses. This will boost your confidence.

5b.8   Live by your values

I have saved this part to the last because when you eat a plate of food you should, as a dear love of mine once told me, savour the best part last. Living by your values is one of the things that in my experience is the key to finding out why you are unhappy in any given situation.

Once you have defined your values using self-awareness, you will see why certain things just aren't working out for you. Say for example one of your core values is integrity. Your colleague at work is very short of money and cannot afford to pay her rent that month. You see she has taken money from the company. This would sit uncomfortably with you as your core value is integrity. However, a person whose core value is loyalty may consider the colleague to be more important and sit on the side of their friend who is struggling.

This is not a discussion on what is right or wrong at this point, but is about understanding ourselves as individuals and therefore managing ourselves better through our values. Also use the mission statement exercise in Appendix 8.5.

The question is why we become so upset about things going on externally to ourselves, and how do we better manage that?

The answer is to keep checking in with your values. When you feel uncomfortable about a situation, remind yourself of these questions: 'Am I living by my values? What values am I not living up to right now?'

Consider the following scenario.
"I observe Bob being particularly unkind to Jan at work. He starts picking on her inability to generate sales and I can see that Jan is taken aback by it. She seemed for the rest of the day very withdrawn. I know that

I am lacking in confidence and am actively working on it. I know I should have said something but it was too late and Bob has the ear of the boss and can be a bit of a bully at times, but he hasn't turned on me so I don't want to attract attention to myself.

I go home and can't sleep, I feel terrible, I write a text to Jan saying I hope she's ok, but again that only relieves the uncomfortable feeling for a little while. I don't want to say in the message that Bob was wrong in case he sees the message or I get into trouble.

I have seen what he is capable of, what he has done to others and its really affecting me. There are others in the office who are not affected by Bob and just say, 'oh that's just Bob', and they appear to move on. I don't know why it is affecting me so much."

This person's values are kindness, loyalty and integrity. While the person is not being directly unkind, in the mix of their own personal values, they are not meeting any of them. They are not being loyal to those people in the office they call friends, nor are they speaking their truth about the behaviour.

We feel uncomfortable, bad or unhappy or all of them when we are not being true to ourselves or our values.

ACTION

Keeping your values near you and reminding yourself of them is really important. Here are some ways to keep them near you and at the forefront of your mind:

- Put your values into a poster, frame it to put on the wall, maybe on your desk.
- Even just sticking a post-it note on your computer will keep your values in your line of sight.
- A screen saver on your computer or phone with your values on them.
- A daily reminder that pops up to check you in with them.

Whichever way you choose to remind yourself of your values, be sure to hold them dear to you and you will always be able to manage your reactions much better.

5c   Social Awareness

Social awareness is all about the ability to understand and respond to the needs of other people.   Here we discuss the ideas on how you can improve this ability.

5c.1   Learn to listen

How hard is it to listen?

It really challenges your shadow ego, smaller self in us. To be truly present we have to release all that ego structure that it is telling us to be. Superiority, separation and in the micro-moment prioritise the communion over our need to be right or our need to impose an objective and especially when that person starts telling us stuff we don't like or that we disagree with. It takes a bit of discipline but there is a beautiful shift that happens, it is like you put on different glasses. I start to see differently though a different lens, it makes it more difficult to judge because I hope I am beginning to see people more completely as I start to see myself more completely. When we do that, it's hard not to be kind to each other. At that point it takes more effort to be unkind to each other. If I am willing to see my shadow and wholeness, then I have a greater solidarity with others in our stories.

Benjamin Mathes, Founder at Urban Confessional

Social awareness is understanding how people are reacting to us and how we are supporting them. Learning to listen is absolutely key to this but this is much easier said than done. Everyone thinks they are good listeners however active listeners are really very conscious about it. Not interrupting and not talking about self as a comparison when someone is sharing something of themselves. We want to share our own stories to show we understand but so often we can take over a situation if we don't draw it back to the person's story quite quickly to demonstrate we are listening and are really present with someone.

Listening is a key to many parts of this book and is at the heart of making a culture of kindness. To be a great leader you must first have the ability to listen. Listen to your stakeholders, including your staff, peers, competition and customers to name a few. If you cannot really listen and be present to understand through careful and considered questioning on all the things you might not understand, then you will not be a successful leader. I am not usually as bold with my statements but I can stand up and debate this quite happily to anyone who believes that not listening makes you a good leader.

However great listening is often tough with all the other pressures within the workplace. As new situations develop it can quickly feel too busy to listen to someone's story. However, when you make time for brilliant listening you will find the rewards are unlimited. They include loyalty, more productivity, better employee engagement, employee happiness, employee retention to name but a few.

Let's look at some actions to improve listening for you and your teams.

Practice great listening. Do this on your own by making sure you make time to listen to colleagues, but also practice in your day-to-day interactions. If you realise you are not naturally a gifted listener then take the actions as though you are in a play, the character you are playing is an exceptional listener and undertakes the characteristics as mentioned below with ease. From here it will give you a starting ground to improve your listening skills. You can also get your teams role-playing. Act it out and you will become it.

A Culture of Kindness

Maintain eye contact. This might seem simple, but our eye gets easily distracted in an office. Our phone might ping. We might watch something through the window. We may even simply feel a little less confident that day such that full on eye contact with someone just feels too much. However, you must become the actor, inhabit the role of holding the right amount of eye contact.

No judgement. Whatever a person is sharing with you, to truly listen you must do so without judgement. Judging people can be seen in your body language. If something they say shocks you, it is fine to feel shocked, but don't allow yourself to say anything in your head like, 'Well, I can't believe you did that.' As soon as you indulge in judgmental inner thoughts, you've compromised your effectiveness as a listener.

Listen without jumping to conclusions. Remember that the speaker is using language to represent the thoughts and feelings inside their brain. You don't know what those thoughts and feelings are, so the only way you'll find out is by listening.

Build the picture. NLP provides a trick to help you remember people's names. When a person introduces themselves, in your mind's eye imagine drawing their name on their forehead. The idea is it plants an image of their name whenever you see them. The same idea can be utilised when listening to a story, by building a picture of what is being communicated. If someone is talking about a situation, picture it as they describe it. This is also great for building empathy specifically for emotional situations for the sharer. Having empathy and putting yourself in someone's shoes is key to great listening as outlined in the chapters that follow.

Don't interrupt. It goes without saying, but don't interrupt. All it says to the person is, 'You are not important'. It is sometimes so tough when you want to comfort someone or really engage in their story by adding to it. In all my time of talking and even evaluating myself as a listener, I have only seen one person do this extremely well time and time again. She had clearly worked on herself and her listening skills so well it was extremely noticeable that she was with me on the story I was sharing.

Practice. Keep practising and working on listening better with every interaction you have.

Don't fix it. We all want to fix things for people, make it better for them. People will ask for advice if they want it. If you think they might want advice or that you have a brilliant solution that cannot be kept to yourself, ask them first.

Question only for clarity on the topic. This is so easily done. For example, someone is talking about the events of their birthday when they mention their grandmother and I say, 'Oh yes, How is she?' and we move the conversation onto how their grandmother is, rather than allowing the person to share the whole story about their birthday. Questions should only have included asking questions that build clarity, such as confirming the venue for the birthday dinner. If you inadvertently do this, make sure you are conscientious enough to recognise the need to bring the conversation back to the birthday.

Feedback. Show that you understand where the speaker is coming from by reflecting their feelings back, 'Wow you must be pleased', or 'That must be tough right now.' If you are unsure then confirm through nods, facial expressions or sounds of agreement or acceptance. This gives the speaker confidence you are listening to them.

Body language. Much of our conversation is had non-verbally. We can understand a lot through tone and pitch, the second silence. When face to face, we can detect a whole range of emotions by positioning, facial expression, eye contact and simply how a person holds themselves. When listening to someone words are just a very small part of the story.

ACTION

At work and at home over the next 30 days you must ensure that at the end of your conversations you summarise what was said. This is to start to practice your ability to listen. Do this particularly over task-orientated things. The only way to improve your listening skills is to practice them.

5c.2   What is someone else feeling?

Compassion and empathy are different
Empathy is deeper of the heart than compassion.
Empathy is about seeing the world from someone else's eyes, can you
imagine their own suffering.
Mere compassion you notice and you wish it would be taken away.

The capacity to see someone else's eyes is helpful and stops your own
selfishness.

Emma Slade, Founder of 'Opening your heart to Bhutan'

Although empathy is covered in more depth later in the book (see Chapter 6.4), it deserves its own section here. There is a person at work, maybe it's your boss who is closed off to pleasant interaction and comes across as being a little unpleasant. You aren't sure where they are coming from and you really want to ask but you have no idea of the correct approach. This is where understanding what it is like to be in their shoes is your golden nugget. This method is used to try and understand what they are feeling in a meeting. (Here I will add a disclaimer, the best way to truly find out how someone is feeling is to ask questions, listen well and build long-term relationships through more obvious and immediate forms of empathy building.) However, as a general tool to understand someone better, this is great.

Have you ever imagined being in someone else's shoes, really sat and spent time thinking about it? Wondering what life they have at home, the pressures they have outside work, or even the pressures that they face at work? How someone really felt when their wife left them, or why they are in an abusive relationship and the reasons they don't want to leave? Tuning into people not only means we listen more when they speak but we can more easily understand what it is like being in their shoes, which allows us to grow in empathy. Every company should consider holding more social events at which people share stories. That way people will better understand each other's perspectives.

ACTION

Take the physical action to step into someone else's shoes. This does not mean literally taking their shoes from them. Simply stand up in a space that gives a metre space around you and close your eyes. On the floor by your side, imagine an empty pair of shoes and the person who owns them. Have a very clear image of them in your mind's eye.

Then take a physical step to step into the shoes you have imagined. From there you should imagine what their day is like. The pressures, the highs and lows, what might motivate them and what might make them sad. And so on. This imaginary role allows us to understand how a person might feel.

The exercise would allow you to understand from another viewpoint and potentially grow your empathy levels. You may not always be accurate, the importance is that it stretches the empathy muscle to help it grow. You will get more attuned to doing this. When we understand others we can then attempt to understand them and in turn work with them more cooperatively.

5c.3   Acceptance

Different countries have a different lens on; with regards to diversity and inclusion.

Sean Tompkins, Global CEO, RICs

The world is moving to one of acceptance. Not everywhere just yet, however it's the direction of travel, and if you have not already adopted an accepting mindset, it's something to very quickly learn. Social awareness is dead in the water without learning to accept everyone for who they are.

Acceptance is not simply a behaviour automatically learnt in childhood. It may be that employees can be helped to be more accepting of others using education or training. By this I do not mean just send them on a course and tick a box. Instead I am talking about deep communication, sharing and exploring vulnerability to allow people to truly feel someone else's story in a safe environment.

Empowerment within a team is often discussed but in reality is not always given. However, for a person to have the freedom to be creative and ultimately deliver original and award-winning service or products, they need to have freedom. It can be daunting for a manager to give staff freedom, but it all starts with acceptance. Sharing personal stories in a safe setting of acceptance starts ripples of understanding.

ACTION

Start a way to share stories. There are some excellent initiatives that allow you to hear people's stories, such as the human library, or bringing diverse speakers into the workplace to create a more open-minded atmosphere.

5c.4 Networking

Networking should ultimately be thought of as making new relationships, or reinforcing existing ones. It is no longer about handing over a business card, but about investing time and really knowing someone.

Practice makes perfect. Being around people practising the skills you have learnt to listen, demonstrate empathy and improve communication with others can only really be achieved by repetition. With the ease with which we can network through technology it can be challenging for some to push themselves to go out and network outside of that. Some people are born with the skills to network, others have to learn this over time. In addition, networking is usually not taught within a work environment, but it is expected that we should just know how to do it.

Each networking group has its own dynamics, there are challenges to navigate therefore when joining a group. These include the traditions and rules of engagement they may have, the already established relationships and the need to build trust with other networkers for mutual benefit.

Networking is most successful where you have similar wants, desires or interests. If you are going into a networking group and your values and plans for the future are not at the forefront of your mind, then it's likely networking will be unsuccessful.

Of course, networking will help your career but it will also increase your social awareness scores on your EQ and allow you to grow and develop on an overall level. The more we do something the more we get used to it and that it helps us to build confidence. You or a member of your team might not possess the natural instinct to network but the only way we gain those skills is to expose ourselves to situations where we can learn them. It also allows us to practice our listening skills, gain new ideas, new opportunities may present themselves for us to flourish and you get a sounding board for your own future ideas. The act of networking, particularly face-to-face, has never been so important in a world turning to technology.

ACTION

If you really want to develop your people, designing a course on networking which demonstrates methods to network is hugely important. Individuals need to join clubs and networking groups. You can find these through many social media groups including Meet-up. (42) Maybe start with joining a particular group, such as a book club, a speakers club or cycling club depending on your interests. Choose something that will grow your skills and knowledge but allow you to network in a comfortable environment. The idea of networking by approaching a stranger can be daunting, however the answer lies in what you will have at your fingertips. You should have in your pocket a couple of questions that will provoke an open response that allows conversation to start.

Example questions
What do you do?
What are the parts of your role you really love?
What do you like to do in your time outside of work?

A Culture of Kindness

5c.5   Conflict resolution

*Life is transformational not transactional. The more we ask questions
rather than impose answers, the more we will seek understanding instead
of seeking to being right. I don't even have to like you, but I can try and
understand you.*

Benjamin Mathes, Founder of Urban Confessional

Conflict simply means groups or individuals having different goals or/
and opinions, which, if unresolved, have the potential to prevent an
individual or group achieving their aims. Obviously, if war breaks out in
your work environment it probably means that some additional work is
needed to increase your social awareness. While I make jest of it, in fact
the inability to resolve conflict means you probably need to start going
through the exercises to support yourself and increase social awareness.
You need to be more in tune with people who have differing opinions,
which means thinking more kindly towards others. You might feel
frustrated, but those listening skills are more important than ever now.

Let's look at the main sources of conflict as proposed by American
psychologist Daniel Katz. (43) According to him, conflict arises primarily
due to three things:

Economic conflict. This occurs due to a limited amount of resources.
The groups or individuals involved come into conflict in competition for
these resources, thus bringing forth hostile behaviours among those
involved.

Value conflict. This concerns conflict between the varied preferences
and ideologies held by different individuals or groups. Conflicts driven by
this factor give rise to wars whereby separate parties have sets of beliefs
that they assert in an aggressive manner.

Power conflict. This occurs when the parties involved intend to maximise their influence. Such a situation can happen among individuals, groups or even nations. In other types of conflict, power is also evident as it involves asserting influence over another.

Below are some of the impacts of not being able to manage conflict:
Poor relationships
Resentment
Poor wellbeing
Low productivity
Unresolved and simmering problems

Conversely, managing conflict well can bring:
Even better relationships than previously
Improved communication
Efficient problem solving
Higher productivity
Great teamwork

I know which environment I would prefer to work in. If we can learn to handle conflict in a constructive manner, we can then appreciate that conflict does not need to be destructive but can in fact help us to grow. It can lead to a healthy sharing of ideas and opinions and allow us to accommodate new concepts and ideas. It should be understood that conflict is a natural part of life, and without it, we would not challenge each other to do or be better, but would passively accept what is dished out to us, like robots! More often than not, it's not the conflict that is the problem, but how we choose to deal with it that brings us negative results and damaged relationships.

Most of us have learned to view conflict as an unpleasant thing. However, conflict is simply how people think and behave according to their differing backgrounds and circumstances. It also occurs in response to frustration, and possibly as an expression of aggressive and competitive instincts. Inner conflicts reflect our difficulties in coming to terms with life's challenges or in accepting ourselves as we truly are (this does not mean that we must put up with how we are!)

The most valuable aspect of conflict is the energy that it generates. Conflict management is not an attempt to suppress this energy, but to use it constructively. Conflict can lead to harsh and painful situations, or it can be transformed into wonderful, creative and productive conversations that move things forwards positively. It will become easier to manage if we see it as part of the journey but that it does not need to be destructive, and as a problem to be solved rather than a battle to be won.

Top tips on conflict management

See that the person and the problem are different things. Separating the person who you may feel is at the heart of the conflict from the problem that is being disputed will help you to see it much less personally. You will then be able to resolve the conflict and support the person without judgement.

Language. As with NLP, remember that you need to consider the effects of the language you use on a given situation.

Acceptance. Conflict has to happen. When we accept it as part of the growth process we can choose to resolve the challenges rather than block them which is counter-productive.

Listen. This is a constant process. Kindness is listening, and giving time to someone, really is at the heart of this whole book.

Calm. You may or may not be connected to the problem or have feelings about the person. However, it is important to put them aside, find a place of calmness to resolve the conflict. The mindfulness techniques will help with this.

Focus on the future. It is easy for a conflict to keep circulating while the discussion stays on the past or on a point that will never change. Focusing on a way to move forward will break the cycle.

ACTION

Observe in your workplace the different types of conflict which typically occur and how other people generally react to that. What type of conflict is most prevalent – Economic, Value, Power? How do you personally react to that conflict? Take notes of your main observations. How does this differ from conflict you see in other areas of your personal life? Again, record your observations. It can be useful to make a comparison table which details your observations and comparisons.

5c.6 Communication skills

A key skill that is so important for leadership and kindness is listening. So, if you are only on email you are not using that skill. To develop your EQ and utilise it, you have to use those listening skills.

Emma Sergeant, President Europe, DAS Group of Companies (a division of Omnicom)

Increasing our communication skills and the ability to communicate effectively to all sections of society is a hugely important part of social awareness. Let me be clear when I talk about 'the sections of society'. When I do a talk to school children my communication is very different to that when I am talking to a room of CEOs, even though my topic or story could well be the same. The variety and differences within our society needs to be considered when we are communicating, otherwise the message will simply be lost or ignored.

Although some of you may believe this to be obvious, being able to judge this choice of communication is not only kind, it is emotionally intelligent and also very important to grow successfully yourself. We should not all assume we are very good at it without some consideration.

For example, after completing the 'Your roles' exercise, you will better understand who you are to each person. This is an extremely valuable exercise in the importance of how much we adapt our communication to meet each need. If you come into your PR office communicating in your father role you might be considered condescending. Defining the roles will certainly help with ongoing communication practices.

Communication is studied in its own right, so we will not be able to cover all the nuances here. Our aim is to look at communication from a perspective of growing your social awareness and therefore making a culture of kindness. This is not simply about how you communicate but also understanding how that communication is received. For example, if you are delivering a speech and if someone has dozed off, it is likely that the room is too warm or you need to communicate differently with more inflection and tonal variety. What about though the tiny signs that the audience has not understood your point, or if a humorous moment is lost? Being able to adapt on the spot in those situations is often a challenge for many, however when you are talking and sharing with colleagues that is not usually the case. The power to adapt our communication to suit the listener is all about reading them.

If you've ever tried to hide your feelings, you probably realised very quickly that it's pretty hard to do. I know that my face moves before I can stop it, and I am honest by default as my face tells the story before I can speak the words, I'd make a terrible poker player! Our feelings play a huge part in the way we communicate. If we're angry, sad, or afraid, we may well be able to control our verbal communication, but not so much the nonverbal cues. This is where emotional awareness, or the ability to understand and communicate our feelings, will help. If you are emotionally aware, you will take the time to notice the emotions of other people and how their feelings influence the way they communicate. Whether it's helping an anxious employee cope with stress or convincing your boss to give you the promotion/raise you feel you deserve, you need to be able to gauge the situation, adapt as needed over the course of the interaction, and then be ready to come to some type of satisfactory resolution. If your boss doesn't seem to be in the mood to talk about that promotion, you need to be aware enough to determine the best time to engage in that discussion.

Interpersonal communication. The ability to form relationships and deal with the people around you.

Intrapersonal communication. The communication that you have internally through language and thought.

Certain CEOs exhibit interesting communication practices. For example, the view that digital slideshow presentations is old news. Steve Jobs instituted a rule at Apple that banned all these type of presentations. Sheryl Sandberg did likewise at Facebook. Both leaders realised that slideshow presentations can hinder rather than help communication.

Before the age of technology and long before that, we would share news through storytelling, meaning local people sharing stories in the street. It remains today the most powerful way to communicate by employing compelling stories and non-verbal cues to convey your point to the audience. Storytelling may well be the secret that builds empathy and grows connections. Storytelling is another way that we can be kind. Sanjiv Nichani, Founder of the Healing Hearts Foundation, among others I asked said that their kindness came from the way they had been brought up, and stories they were told. *I was brought up with great kindness and taken it the other way and taken advantage of that. My grandmother used to tell me stories, mythological stories that embedded into my brain.*

Non-verbal communication makes up about 55 percent of communication. That means getting comfortable with being expressive. If you are trying to explain the benefits of your new idea to the workplace but you sit slumped with your head in your hands, you are unlikely to inspire your listener to buy into the idea. As previously discussed also, eye contact when we listen is an essential part of communication.

It has been said that we have to over-communicate just to communicate and I have seen this first-hand in most businesses I have worked within. We so often assume that people will know what we know.

In 1990, a graduate student at Stanford University (44) was able to prove that presenters overestimate how much listeners understand. In a study that became known as 'the tappers and the listeners', one set of participants was asked to tap the melody of 120 famous songs. The other participants were asked to guess what song was being tapped. Tappers estimated that 50 percent of the songs tapped would be correctly identified. In reality, only 2.5 percent of songs were correctly identified. This study shows that it is important to communicate clearly, and to over-communicate when sharing new ideas. As this study indicates, it is likely that the audience will fail to absorb as much as you might expect.

Knowing who it is you are communicating to is really helpful. If you are giving a talk to 500 strangers this might be trickier. However, in the workplace, understanding your teams, what they value, their key drivers and so forth will help you to adapt your communications to match them.

Listening
You must first listen more than you speak to communicate best with your teams. Ask for feedback on your communications, checking whether your point is understood in the way you intended.

As with most leadership skills, receiving honest feedback from colleagues, managers and members of your team is critical to becoming a better communicator. If you regularly ask for feedback, others will help you to discover areas for improvement that you might have otherwise overlooked

Communicating clearly is one of the most effective skills you can cultivate as a business leader. Remember to communicate using non-verbal and verbal cues. Listen carefully to what others have to say, and over-communicate in novel ways to ensure the content of the conversation sticks with the audience.

ACTION

Think about your language, your non-verbal communication, tone and inflection. Consider the reactions of those you are communicating, and start to evaluate how you can adapt your communications skills to better support the people around you

.

5d   Relationship management

*Human nature and action should be able to look out for other people.
People need help in all shapes and walks of life. Everyone needs an arm
around them at some point. The default human nature must be kindness
and if we can install that kindness into the culture and deliver it, make sure
we can be kind, help someone, share your bag of crisps, ask someone how
they are; the world would be a different place. If you pay it forwards you
will always get it back.*

PJ Ellis, Co-owner of Lightbox Digital

All the other skills build into this last EI skill. You need the other three
for this to fall into place. This is your last and final wall to the house.

5d.1   Influence: persuading others

The secret to many success stories lies in persuading others to come on
board with an idea. Influence and manipulation can so often be confused
but people very quickly feel the difference between the two. Manipulation
is defined as having control over others in a way that benefits the
manipulator. Influence might seem similar, but it lacks the negative
connotations. A manipulator gains control through fear, greed or guilt and
those being manipulated will feel pressured and trapped as it is unlikely to
be of any benefit to them.

Interestingly the word 'influence' has an ancient root in the Middle
English word meaning 'emanation of the stars', and 'the emanation of
moral or spiritual force'. People who are influential tend to
be charismatic and admirable. We are inspired by them and aspire to be

like them. We feel good around them. When we think of manipulation we think of the negative and when we think of influence we think of good. Influence ultimately allows things to happen and achieve desired outcomes.

Compared to manipulation, influence takes into consideration others' needs and desires. As a parent we might want to influence our children to be healthy and safe because we understand that is good for them. As friends, we want to influence our friends to happy and fulfilled. As leaders, we want to influence our staff to be happy and content within their work.

Influence has many components. It's based on strong connections, trust, good communication, and awareness and acceptance of others which we have learned in Chapters 5c.1, 5c.3 and 5c.6. Improving in these skills should positively affect your ability to influence. Once you can do this well, it will help you to bring people on board with the culture of kindness you are building, based on similar values and goals. It will help to ensure people do not work against those objectives also.

If you are not a leader you can still use influence to present your case and work together collaboratively to convey your goals and what support you require. Influencing tactics fall into three categories:
logical (head)
emotional(heart)
cooperative (hands)

Logical appeals tap into people's rational and intellectual positions. You present an argument for the best choice of action based on organisational or personal benefits, or both.

Emotional appeals connect your message, goal, or project to individual goals and values. An idea that promotes a person's feelings of wellbeing, service, or sense of belonging has a good chance of gaining support.

Cooperative appeals involve collaboration (what will you do together?), consultation (what ideas do other people have?), and alliances (who already supports you or has the credibility you need?). Working together to accomplish a mutually important goal extends a hand to others in the organisation and is an extremely effective way of influencing.

So how do you want to tackle things? Start with some strategies on how to build a culture you can influence.

Trust. We talk about this as the value later on (see Chapter 6.2). You will gain trust from people you work with by being honest, admitting to your mistakes and shortcomings, revealing who you are and that you have your colleagues' backs. It's simple really, they will in turn have yours.

Consistency. Being consistent happens when all of your team buy into the organisational morals. It sets the standard for how not only staff, but leaders will behave. By being consistent with rewards and praise, people feel secure in a place that is predictable and they will come to rely on a solid and strong leadership style. This makes them more receptive to positive influence.

Listening. The ability to take into account other people's thoughts or ideas will immediately get them on board. You must actually consider what they tell you and be willing to make adjustments accordingly. If you are rigid it will limit the likelihood of wielding any influence. If you are unable to be flexible be prepared to work on how you deliver that and provide good reasons for your decision. Reiterate that you have heard the ideas, explaining why in this instance you are unable to accommodate them.

Approachable. You need to be approachable as a leader and a colleague. The hierarchy leadership has gone. We must talk, be kind and considerate to our colleagues and teams. If people can't speak they will retreat, and you won't be able to influence them if you can't get to know them. It's important to share some of yourself so that they know who you are.

Be kind. You do not need to shout or be dictatorial to get your message across. Assertiveness comes from confidence, good communication and a passion for your subject. Your message should always be in line with the interests of colleagues, wider society or the environment so communicating it can be assertive without any aggression. To overcome any objections it's important to listen more and talk less, and to do so graciously.

Fewer words, more actions. As previously discussed, organisational morals set out what actions are considered acceptable for a cohesive working environment, and of course they must be based on being kind. This means actively creating a culture that allows everyone to come to work and enjoy what they do. This action requires more than just the CEO lecturing employees, it is the beating heart of the organisation. Action speaks louder than words when it comes to influence.

5d.2 Inspirational leadership: providing a vision that motivates

You have to inspire other people to engage in a particular way. So, if you have a passion for something your leadership must help them to understand the opportunities but also how to engage into that. For example, you have HR and Finance etc you are trying to share the vision but show how you make it possible across all the divisions. People want to be inspired and engaged in something. Culture and people make success.

Phil Smith, Chairman at IQE, Prev. CEO, Cisco

Employees need to feel some inspiration from their work, something that gives them get up and go. Teams become more productive with inspiration and, as with kindness, it is contagious.

Bain and company have published several pieces of research. (45) (46) The results show some great opportunities for leaders to inspire as, according to the research, inspirational leaders are 'made and not born'.

Sadly, the research found that less than half of respondents said they agree or strongly agree that their leaders were inspiring or were unlocking motivation in employees. Even fewer felt that their leaders fostered engagement or commitment and modelled the culture and values of the organisation.

They then completed a survey of 2,000 people. The findings were interesting. They said inspiration alone was not enough, nor was just focusing on performance or any one individual part of leadership. However, they had discovered that, by focusing on the strengths of the leaders, employees were more likely to view them as inspirational. It meant the team appeared to back the leader and made the team stronger because of it. This happened because of 'empowerment, not command and control'.

The overall results reported several strengths within leaders that caused teams to feel inspired. The great news was you only need one of the 33 to actually inspire teams.

Developing inner resources - Stress tolerance, self-regard, emotional self-awareness, flexibility, independence, emotional expressionism, self-actualisation and optimism

Connecting with others - Vitality, humility, empathy, development, assertiveness, listening, expressiveness and commonality

Setting the tone - World view, balance, shared ambition, follow through, recognition, openness, unselfishness, balance and responsibility

Leading the team - Empowerment, co-creation, vision, harmony, direction, focus, servanthood, and sponsorship

Having one of these strengths and being seen as the best in that trait within your peer group gave the leader twice the chance of being seen as an inspirational leader. As you can imagine as you cast your eye over the 33 strengths, the people who were thus 'inspirational' were incredibly diverse.

However, there was one strength that indicated matters more than any other: **centeredness**. As the authors put it, *This is a state of mindfulness that enables leaders to remain calm under stress, empathise, listen deeply, and remain present.* Everything that we have discussed throughout this book so far are all key factors.

However, as we have seen, your key strength has to match how your organisation is founded. Which, when you look at the 33 traits, is hard not to connect with any organisational morals, purpose or vision that may be had.

Effective leadership isn't generic. To achieve great performance, companies need a leadership profile that reflects their unique context, strategy, business model, and culture, the company's unique behavioural signature. To win in the market, every company must emphasise the specific capabilities that make it better than the competition.

Interestingly, they also found the most inspirational leaders 'spiky' not well-rounded, and the 'spikes' must be relevant to the way the organisation functions and its vision and values. This is all about being able to focus on our strengths and really matching ourselves into the work that is right for our own values.

For example, an organisation that is focused on creativity is likely to be inspired by a leader whose core strength is co-creation.

You have to behave differently if you want your employees to do so too, to inspire is sometimes being brave enough to challenge the norm. Stretching our own abilities to show that anything is possible is always an inspiring story. To lead we must understand that is the mindset to adopt. We focus on strengths which you must seek out in your team, giving them a chance to inspire your organisation.

Inspirational leaders can often find a great individual opportunity or moment to increase performance culture in a way that can also be inspiring. These are real moments of leadership and truth.

When Howard Schultz returned to Starbucks as CEO after a long break, he realised that Starbucks was no longer the front runner for best coffee experience. *In the front seat were automation and diversification, both implemented in pursuit of throughput and growth.* Schultz took dramatic action that to some may have seemed risky but he shut down 7,100 US stores for 3 hours in 2008, to retrain the baristas in the art of making espresso. In this bold move, he made it clear that there was nothing he would not do to make Starbucks great again.

A Culture of Kindness

When Alan Mulally came to Ford in 2006 to help turn the business around, he took bold actions to change the way the company operated. In one highly visible moment, he applauded Mark Fields (who would eventually become his successor) for admitting to a failure in an executive meeting. That was pretty much unheard-of at Ford, and it set the tone for the open and honest communications required for a new culture at the company.

Drawing insight from Eastern philosophy, if you want to change the way of being, you have to change the way of doing. Leaders can only change by doing things differently. The more often they behave in a new way, the sooner they become a new type of leader, an inspirational leader.

Self-awareness is the key to understanding our weak points, but as already suggested, maybe we should focus on our strengths. A growing body of research indicates that encouraging people to bolster their strengths is more effective than working on weaknesses. According to Gallup research, (47) 73 percent of employees report being engaged with their organisation when its leadership focuses on the strengths of its employees, compared with 9 percent when they do not.

One of the things we know is that when things are negative, people see fewer options, [and] *they're less able to problem solve. It shuts down the brain,* said business psychologist Jennifer Thompson, an associate professor at the Chicago School of Professional Psychology. *When people have positive environments, they're more creative. They're more productive.* (48)

An inspirational leader is driven by a set of core values that they live and breathe by. To inspire they must project mutual trust, which we have mentioned is essential for building a culture of kindness, but also the ability to lead by demonstrating those values. Leaders naturally have the ability to coach, give guidance and empower their teams.

A white paper by Lucy Finney, MBE, discusses the six key elements for inspiring your staff. She talks about how Steven Covey (author, speaker and thought leader on leadership) describes how trust must lie at the heart of inspiration, and that trust is a mixture of character and competence. (49)

Leaders give coaching and empower through teams and in turn they gain loyalty by leading with their values. *Inspirational leadership should be thought of as a leadership ethos that creates a climate where teams and individuals flourish. The climate people work in stimulates aligned action towards successful outcomes, people feel empowered, teaming is visible, enthusiasm is present and individuals are committed to the success of the organisation.*

We are all seeking to be inspired in one way or another. Valeria Locatelli from M&G Prudential, whom I interviewed for the podcast is a wonderful unique example who has set up a monthly book club. She invites speakers to talk about their books, allowing employees and guests to learn and network at the same time. There is no personal gain just a desire to inspire others.

Some of our most powerful moments in history are from speeches. I can still remember Barack Obama's 'Fired up, ready to go' speech'. I used to show my teams that speech as the ending says so much, that we might only be individuals, but if we come together we have the power to change the world. He is a storyteller, and as we know, good storytellers are great influencers. They draw on the emotions of the listener, which is a powerful skill when delivering speeches.

What Obama demonstrated so much in his time in office was that he shared who he was, he was transparent, confident, honest and relatable. He admitted when he made a mistake, he said when his hands were tied. His values led the way he worked, and we could see his intentions along with his values were driven only by goodness. When we are ourselves and focus on our key strengths, we naturally inspire others.

5d.3 Developing others: providing feedback, skills and knowledge

It's looking after the people who work for you, not the people who work for you looking after you. So, if you manage them, you must think, how am I going to support the people to be better, to be more supportive, be happier; that generates a more positive working environment.

Lord Mark Price, Founder of Engaging Works, former Deputy Chairman of The John Lewis Partnership and Managing Director of Waitrose.

When we understand ourselves and what makes us grow we can objectively give feedback. Understanding how our communication is being and might be interpreted is also key. Returning to our 'culture of kindness' house metaphor, once you have built the walls based on awareness, acceptance and communication, you can start to build the roof with ease.

Developing others is a gift and an honour. Protect it carefully, as well as those you are developing. This is kindness encompassed.

After collecting data from more than 400,000 employees, the company Zenger Folkman discovered that opportunity for individual development was the third most significant driver of employee engagement. In additional to pay and benefits, developing new skills is viewed as a very important benefit by most employees.

From this they looked at what leaders did well to promote this and arrived at four key development areas.
1. Focus on performance management
2. Involve your team
3. Recognition
4. The job fits the person

My guidance on these points is simple. We have already covered a good deal on them, but please allow me to expand slightly on what has gone before.

Focus on performance management, absolutely yes. But if you are crunching numbers you are not getting to the heart of the person. Without that you might as well hire robots. People have human needs, they need to have conversation and human connection. If you only focus on the task at hand you are likely to lower the performance management. The essential take away here is that performance management is not restricted to a six monthly or yearly review. It is something you should be doing constantly, and not just as a chat about tasks. I have included a performance management proforma in Appendix 8.9 help you build a culture of kindness and to back up the theory behind the book. Consider also what their hopes and dreams are, allow them to be honest. It might be to travel the world, but employees might be too nervous to tell their employers that for fear of being pushed out. Support your employees' dreams as it will encourage loyalty but also because they are more than robots, they are humans.

Involving your team. I have covered this in previous parts of the book but it would be helpful to briefly summarise here. Why hire people as experts in their field and then not involve them? You will struggle to make much work without employee buy-in, but when do they buy in? When they have designed it!

Recognition, we all need to be seen. It's a human condition to be recognised and appreciated for what we have done. If we work all day every day and never get an acknowledgement we wonder if it is worth it. Conversely, the more we recognise effort, the more people will want to do.

The job fits the person. If I take you back to the two guys doing the same job but who had different values; this part relates to that. We always need to focus on a person's strengths rather than focus on trying to squeeze that round peg into the square hole, it's just painful for them and frustrating for the leader.

5d.4 Change catalyst: recognising the need for change and supporting the process

In my HR role I have had to be the organisation's conscience and I have quite often had to encourage more senior leaders to think about the pace in which they are trying to implement organisational change and develop enough stuff into the change programs so that we are bringing people with us. That is a challenge with profit warnings and a drive to make change really quickly to save a corporate entity. I have always tried to strike a balance between what is important for the business and the people. However, bringing people along on the journey in a kind and caring way, explaining and re-explaining about why things are happening.

Pippa Richardson, Director, The Head Shed and Shed the Conflict

As leaders we tend to immediately assume people don't want change, however embedding a culture of kindness is going to remove all of those nagging feelings. Most people can cope with change when the values of trust and honesty are adopted within the culture. Change is only seen as negative when there is a simple lack of communication.

Please let me elaborate. Chapter 1.3 introduced the fear state that our brains put us into in modern day situations. All too often this happens because we do not hold all the information we require to evaluate the circumstances and therefore are unable to judge the effect it may or may not have on us. Consequently, we experience fear of the unknown.

When, as a leader we need to make change for the good of the company, whether it affects people or not, that change should be communicated. Remember that the over-communication rule (see Chapter 5c.6) is at its most useful when trying to implement change.

So, when is change needed? It is important that change is not based on a whim, but is truly needed for the greater good. When that is the key driver you are halfway to getting people on board as you can communicate the rationale for change to them clearly. Leaders and people in positions of power can sometimes make change that is led by ego. However, improving your EQ (the walls to your house) will help you not to do this, but also being able to communicate change effectively.

Let's look at examples of change and how different approaches can support this. Say you as a leader want to make changes to current processes, because you can see that they are not working and your research has shown how you can make the system work better. It would be easy to present to the team what you have found, which would give you a sense of accomplishment and possibly praise from your manager.

A kinder alternative would be to explain to the team that you can see the processes are not working, and ask them what they think is not working. What would they like to do differently? How have they envisaged that happening? What are the benefits of change? Do they want to go out and engage with the wider team to see what is suggested? And so on. This will serve you better in the long term.

Recognising there is a need for a change is one thing, how we decide to deliver something is very different. We have the opportunity to engage teams to not only embrace the change but embrace it because they were part of the very design of that change.

How about the much harder process of changing the very structure in which people work? In the most challenging scenario, say the business is not doing so well, making cuts to the structure might be the only way. Or, as a department head you have been told that the staffing budget has been cut. There is no apparent solution in which you can involve the staff.

If this instruction has been given to you, it's very important that you start by drilling into the reasons for the cuts and what other alternatives have been considered. Stand by the intention of kindness, to stand up for your staff and team. You don't have to literally stand up and fight, but you must intend to seek out honesty so you can behave with integrity (more on that later in Chapter 6.3). Due to your excellent emotional intelligence that you have improved through this book, you will manage to get the reasons from your bosses, despite their concerns over affecting shareholder value. You will have already built a culture of kindness in your team I would hope before a scenario like this happens.

At this point, you will do what every other leader would not do. Pull your team together, explain to them you are sharing sensitive information and that you need to have their trust. Explain the situation, and that it is confidential because if the share price drops then the whole company is likely to collapse. Tell them that the staffing budget has had to be cut to survive as it appears to be the last option. However, you want to ask them whether there is something that anyone can think of that could be done to change this? Has anyone got a strategy that will avoid making these cuts? Engage them, allow people to see the problem and, if it truly is the only option, they will also understand that. If cuts are needed, be sure to hold honest and open conversations. Tell them there is not one person they want to lose, but that there may be people in the team that have been considering a change and, if that is the case, support them to make the change to their career or life. This kind of open and honest conversation, while an extreme example, will facilitate change in a much more progressive and kinder way. It will mean less anxiety and stress, people will be happier overall and will support the company out of its difficulties. Of course I make that process appear quite simple, however I understand the complexities, so if you can take the principle of open conversation and over communicating to all not the few, you will make change a more bearable experience for you and those affected by it.

ACTION

Practice. Find something that appears not to be working. Maybe something has scored low in employee engagement surveys. Go in and be honest, say that you want to practice what a good change process looks like in engaging staff and ensuring you as a leader over communicate. Ask them what changes they might deliver to remedy the low scoring issue. Use that as a way to practice making change and also to gain feedback from the team on how they felt throughout the process. You are aiming for less stress and a design that works specifically for you and your business. Doing this also sets the parameters for how your team or business will manage change. This will reduce fear because they will understand the process before major change takes place.

With regard to honesty about the impact on company value for example, if you don't trust your staff you have nothing. Trust will come from trusting. The greatest leaders led with honesty, trust and kindness. For example, Marcus Aurelius was a pioneer in this regard and such a great leader that we still talk about him now nearly 2,000 years later. We have to find our way back to that.

A Culture of Kindness

5d.5 Conflict management: Settling disputes, differences of opinion and misunderstandings

Kindness still pervades the NHS, it is deeply engrained within everyone who works with the NHS, and that's very gratifying. Kindness is however being tainted by all sorts of other things, and sadly if there is not a shift then kindness will start to ebb away. That is, the NHS has not been led properly and a culture of expectations, rights and responsibility has been allowed to develop very rapidly. A blame culture has been allowed to build rapidly. It has been allowed to eat away at the inner core of kindness. The majority of people who work in the NHS want to make a difference but when you are constantly having to watch your back and deal with people who politicians are not honest with. Having to deal with aggressive people you start to lose what is part of you. It becomes a thankless job. We have massive vacancies in the NHS because people are fed up of the culture of expectations. Money will not be the answer but it needs to be managed. The NHS has limitations and those need to be communicated better to the public. I have never seen so many demoralised people.

Sanjiv Nichani, Paediatric heart specialist consultant and founder of Healing Little Hearts Foundation

This has so many facets to it, so let's focus on some key aspects, looking at how the NHS as a system deals with conflict. Then we will consider the conflict that arises when someone doesn't fit the company, asking when is it ok to actually say enough is enough? Lastly, we'll cover what to do when someone leaves the company.

The NHS has been Britain's greatest institution. When we compare systems in other countries, the NHS is free to the user and has saved millions of lives. Harry Smith, who died in November 2018 at the age of

95, spent his retirement advocating the NHS, reminding the world of a time before it. He recalls in one of his most famous speeches the 'anguished cries' of a woman dying from cancer who could not afford morphine, and how his eldest sister had wasted and died of tuberculosis at the age of ten, being 'dumped nameless into a pauper's pit'.

The NHS staff, doctors and nurses are seen by the public as the most trusted professionals and we rely on them almost entirely. They seem godly and we expect more of them than we should of another human. They enter the profession to care for others, but as we know, are not well paid, yet they do it for us, the people. They are however fighting a battle, they are fighting constant cuts to services, based on a political desire to make the NHS profitable. This approach makes health systems in other countries focus on selling drugs rather than on the person, causing over-medication in America for example as a result.

The NHS requires conflict management to deal with the way the nurses and doctors are treated by the public. The public are scared, unwell and ill-informed, and they react accordingly. Talk to most in the NHS and they will tell you that the changes that are needed to make change are deep rooted within its structure. For simplicity we will look at those conflicts where the patient or patient's family becomes aggressive.

It all comes down to listening and over communication. The person needs to be heard, they need action and to understand the challenges faced. The NHS workforce is over-stretched, so sitting with and being able to listen to the person is not always possible if they are in a life-and-death situation. Also, medical professionals are just human, the pressure to keep people alive, to save another and not be affected by a death so that they can still help others is overwhelming. Of course, if members of the public were better able to empathise, that might improve matters for the NHS staff. There is a lot that NHS leaders might do to work on its structure and engage their teams in the process too. While at the heart of the NHS staff there is kindness, from a leadership context there is no culture of kindness. The answer is always honesty, as Sanjiv Nichani highlights in his podcast interview. We must be honest about our limitations. When we understand that we can reduce misunderstanding and limit conflict.

When is enough, enough? When you are a leader, every leadership book tells you how to manage more challenging team members. They explain how you are meant to bow to their needs, which might seem to fit with a culture of kindness. However, that is not what I advocate. Please understand that this doesn't mean I condone the authoritarian leadership approach. I just believe that the 'servant leadership' approach is getting a little lost in translation. Of course, giving people the tools and skills they need is vital, but being a leader is about having those difficult conversations and sometimes saying, this isn't working out, I am not here to serve you, I am here to support you. Supportive leadership would be better but I am not sure it is so catchy as a title.

Servant leadership, might be mistaken for allowing staff to behave in an entitled manner, not address their own issues, and expect to be served. Of course, at the heart of this theory this is not the case or the point that is trying to be made.

Sometimes, an employee just doesn't get it. You have done the performance review, you have tried to highlight in a structured and kind conversation the need to change, suggesting some exercises to undertake to raise their self-awareness. They are just not having it. They blame others for the issues, never address low performance, and the complaints from customers are never due to them, but always someone else. Not many leadership books will say this, but because this is not your usual methodology, I will tell you it's ok to let people go. If people don't want to raise their emotional intelligence for the benefit of the company, the customer and the people that they work with, it's time to say goodbye. We are not servants to the employee, the employee must have a duty of care to not only themselves but to the people they work with.

You may have the smartest person in the entire company on a topic that no one else knows much about, but if they constantly behave in a way that does not fit with the organisational morals, are unkind and make others feel unpleasant, and have no consideration of their own emotional intelligence, then they have to go. This may seem harsh, but that one person will bring the rest of your team down, people will leave, customers also may not come on board, and the overall company growth can be affected by that one person. It is difficult of course to ask someone to leave without clearly setting out the parameters, such as laying out the culture of kindness rules so to speak, but once that is done it is time to see who takes it on board and who believes that they are above such behaviour and values. Zero tolerance doesn't have to be unkind, it has to be about being fair to all. We must to be fair, have gone through the process and attempted to help them build their house in the theory of a culture of kindness. When an employee chooses to reject all that, then is the time to say, I think we need to help you get something more suited for you. Honesty is kindness.

Have you ever been party to the moment when people are asked to leave a company and it's done under a cloud? People pushed out under the cover of darkness never to be heard of again, unless you happen to be on their LinkedIn and see them looking for new work a week later when they have brought themselves round from the humiliation.

There are so many ways people have been exited from a company, leaders who have not done everything they can, but they just have decided the person is out of favour, no longer fits the mould they have made for their company or team. This cannot be allowed to happen in a culture of kindness, it doesn't mean people won't leave in one form or another. However, they must only leave with conversation, honesty, listening and understanding. Too many people are leaving businesses because 'they are

A Culture of Kindness

unhappy', but what exactly is the unhappiness they talk about, they are too nervous to tell anyone so decide to move on instead. This is costly and pointless. An open and honest environment of conversation will combat this and ensure that staff are valued.

When people leave, they must leave because you've tried to help them in themselves and/or found that in fact they are doing work that is not making them happy. Maybe they move within the business, maybe they will change careers or jobs, but to really lead you must support them on that journey on how they will find that. Building the culture of kindness will be key to a change in the way people leave and move between businesses with more dignity and giving other employees hope that they work for a company with integrity and kindness. When that happens you automatically earn loyalty and respect.

This chapter is dedicated to Harry Smith, author and social activist. His death was a sad day for the fight and truth he gave on the change needed in society. Below are some of his thoughts just a few years before his death, after he had spent time in the refugee migrant 'Calais Jungle' and considered the increased use of food banks in the UK. He highlights so well what I hope comes across in this book, that when we focus on money first, no one wins.

I am one of the last few remaining voices left from a generation of men and women who built a better society for our children and grandchildren out of the horrors of the Second World War, as well as the hunger of the Great Depression. Sadly, that world my generation helped build on a foundation of decency and fair play is being swept away by neoliberalism and the greed of the one percent, which has brought discord around the globe. Today, the western world stands at its most dangerous juncture since the 1930s.

5d.6 Building bonds: creating and maintaining networks

When there's a language barrier, kindness seems to become very prevalent as you can't communicate as you usually would. Growing up in a foreign country, it was very obvious amongst my peers who recognised my struggles and wanted to help. They never let the language barrier get in the way. It was a part of my life where I felt incredibly isolated and it was this language of kindness that helped me through.

Amber Dee, Artist/Songwriter

Reciprocity is a wonderful thing when you build a culture, because whatever you do, it will invariably come back to you. So, if you as a leader are uncommunicative, that is likely to come back to you through your staff. Reciprocity of an act is something that tends to happen immediately after. In a brilliant experiment conducted by Phillip Kunz in 1974, (50) he sent 600 Christmas cards depicting himself and his family with a handwritten note. The cards were sent all to strangers and surprisingly, he received 200 cards back. People felt obliged to return the lovely gesture. When we are kind, it makes people feel good and they want to return that favour. While kindness is said to breed kindness, the same can be said of all behaviours and actions, and we naturally without thought reciprocate.

Building bonds with people is all about knowing when and how to engage to not just positively influence the people around you, but to enhance their personal wellbeing. Chapter 5c.4 is about networking and learning how to do that. Networking is not about attending a few networking events, but about learning the art of building bonds with people for the long term. This requires all the skills you have honed such as communication and listening in the earlier stages of emotional intelligence, to really cement those bonds.

Building bonds relates, in my opinion, to the power of being present without having to use words. It means making a person feel valued using small but important actions. Those that know my story know that it was the death of my partner who started me on this journey of kindness. He was absolutely stunning at building bonds with people, he did it consciously but you would imagine it was without effort as it was at the core of his very being. He once told me how importance it was to him that, when he met someone, he would always ask them about themselves, listen and, when he met them again, ensure that he would always ask about the particular topic. If someone was a keen horse rider, he would ask how their horse was and what they had done recently. He was a mad keen football fan so he found that much easier to bond over, but no one was exempt from having to converse with him. If you were caught in a lift with him, he'd have you chatting about your day before you made it to your floor.

Asking people questions and being genuinely interested in their lives is a gift you can easily give. You could write someone a note, give a small gift or homemade goods, but ultimately it, as always, comes down to listening. It is about building people up and supporting them by your presence in the more challenging times. When we build bonds we build trust.

Building bonds has a knock-on effect on your health, it is said to reduce stress and in turn support overall health. It will support your own growth and build community, building bonds has the potential to start ideas that can change society for the better. If we share, care and listen we will develop not only others but also ourselves.

ACTION

By working on the emotional intelligence exercises encountered in this book, building bonds becomes quite natural. To add to this, you can try out Paul's way of building bonds. When you meet someone be sure to find something out about them, be genuinely interested and then when you meet them again be sure to ask them about it. Watch their reaction and take note.

5d.7 Teamwork and collaboration: building effective teams

Kindness is everything in the leadership of schools. As a leader you must believe that kindness will not be abused and that you can manage by exception. What's happened is that people's threat system is up because leaders assume that everyone is not going to do it, they are punitive, they cover every base to cover themselves. There is a lack of trust.

Andy Sammons, Author of the Compassionate Teacher

Compassion is about honesty and being honest with yourself and the other person. This happens a lot in leadership you have to hold your hands up and say you don't have the answer but let us try and get there together. Rather than passing the buck. There is a lack of collaboration. The question I hate is 'what is the impact going to be'. We have become a nation that simply needs to measure everything and there are more subtle and intelligent ways of reflecting on performance. Andy Sammons.

This is the perfect section to end on to build the walls to our culture of kindness house. So much of what we have already discussed brings us back to this, including the establishment of your organisational morals. Having rules of engagement that everyone understands as the way to interact allows people to feel safe and aspire to meet the set of directives.

Those skills, such as intuitively being able to read someone, or behaving in a way that is in line with the values of the company so others will also demonstrate those traits, allow you to promote an environment that listens to others and really responds with thought and discussion.

Team building is not a weekend away doing paint-balling every few years and some fun team activities. In the same way, kindness is not one act and you're done. It is deep-rooted into the everyday activities that make up the interactions of your team. For example, sharing a personal story at a break over the coffee machine with a colleague, and another colleague passing by and giving you a look that they are there for you too when you need them. It's the moments when someone has spiralled into a place they don't know what next to do and four offers of support are given from team members who intuitively see what is happening. It's the moments when a customer's system crashes and your company groups together to get it fixed while you as the leader happen to be on holiday. They are doing it all without you because you made a great team that you facilitated and didn't own.

Some don't encourage the team environment. This is often because of fear, as they need to own the situation and make themselves worthy of the positions they occupy. However, leadership comes when you are constantly trying to make yourself redundant, allowing people to work more collaboratively, more effectively and with consideration for each other.

Managers rarely want to act as mediator in disputes, and when they do, the frustrations felt by those involved frequently cause more anguish. Once again, the key to this is listening. The need to listen and be present even when we might not agree or have an opinion on the matter, is important to building a team. Allow people to learn from you how to act as mediator themselves.

Ask questions all the time, not because you want the answer necessarily, but because you want your team to consider them and ask each other how they can find the answer. Questions should never feel like criticism, or attempts to catch a person out. Not having the answer should be a good thing as it allows the team to work together to find a solution.

A Culture of Kindness

This creates a natural desire for team members to share information with each other. Encourage people all the time to support each other. One person may be very knowledgeable on one topic and might want to do a presentation to share that information. This encourages them to continue to share their knowledge beyond the meeting, makes them feel valued and sets the precedent of sharing information and wisdom.

Giving team members specialism in a topic to be the expert and become the go-to person allows a team to each specialise and recognise that the team is mightier than one person trying to know it all.

It is easy to criticise, to say, 'I don't like that'. It is unproductive and will kill a team and individual in seconds. Criticism can only be given with much more thought and consideration for its long-term effects.

A more constructive approach as I have mentioned, might include only adding ideas to the original idea. For example, if someone is presenting a proposal, the team can only add to the initial plan/proposal in ways that enhance and develop the person's ideas. Those ideas might cover how the plan would positively interact with their own project or department. It could be just an additional service or product that they have heard of that could support the idea to and make it more productive. By only 'adding' in the initial feedback stage, the criticism is led by positivity and therefore productive feedback is given. Each team will need to draw up their own unique rules of engagement on positively reaching consensus in meetings, but it will pay off.

The values in Chapter 6 are essential if people are to understand what core behaviours are expected of them within your team.

We all need to understand what is expected of us, so ensuring that we also have clear goals, job descriptions and objectives for projects is imperative. You'd be surprised how many managers/leaders don't understand that people communicate differently and therefore the objective may not be fully understood. Ensure that everyone is on the same page and that they are comfortable with their contribution to the task at hand. They should as a team split out those tasks on their own without your input. That is when you truly know you have made a great team.

In summary, if you follow the rules of *A Culture of Kindness*, you will indeed have an amazing team that is happy, collaborating and fully engaged.

5d.8   Others second!

So, let's go back to the house. We have not managed to really discuss your team. While I would hope that you understand you are also helping them to build their own 'walls' (Emotional Intelligence) how do they fit within your own house?

Consider that your team, are the doors and windows to the culture of kindness house. Your team should be able to see into your home and understand how you live. You will not have curtains, you are going to demonstrate honesty and vulnerability. Your team should understand what it is like to metaphorically live with you. Each team member is different and needs to be maintained and supported, utilised and cared for just the same as any door or window. They are held in place by the walls, your Emotional Intelligence. If you fail to continue to maintain your own Emotional Intelligence, cracks will start to show within your own structure.

In summary, the doors and windows should be seen as the access points to the leader, that leader should support them by continuing to maintain their 'walls'.

So far you and your teams have been working hard on yourselves, and the result is that your Emotional Intelligence is getting higher. As you will have seen by Chapter 5d on relationship management (wall 4), it starts to all fall into place. Only when you are clear on who you are, can you really support and show up for your teams. When you say, 'This is me', it inspires them with your strengths.

With regard to the culture of kindness house, the foundation is the morals. You have laid the walls by working on yourself, and as long as you maintain them they will stay in good order. Imagine that the people that work for are your windows and doors. You hope to keep them for a long time. But sometimes they will be changed, that's the nature.

The idea is that you can then be there for others by understanding yourself better. If you do this you will take a kinder approach that will motivate, inspire and allow you and your teams to really enjoy the work you are doing.

There will still be things you need to do to support your teams, and the exercises in this book will help you on an ongoing basis.

6.   Seven values to cultivate

I think companies that are genuinely driving authenticity, transparency, integrity, inclusiveness are really actually engaging their people. That they have skin in the game and have an active role in the direction that the company is heading becomes part of the DNA and through leaders and managers and how you hire people then you are really onto a really good thing. So places like Amazon are nailing it.

Pippa Richardson, Director, The Head Shed and Shed The Conflict

Values are hugely important as they represent who someone is. From a company's perspective, values represent what it embodies in their business and their products or services. You could think of it as a stick of rock. If you were a stick of rock, what would the values that were written at your core be, engrained into your very being?

Your company values need to be similarly entrenched, and the way to make sure they are delivered through your teams is to make sure that they match your organisational morals. If you are building the house, you need all the parts to become a whole. If some of those values also match the values of Bain's inspiring leaders (see Chapter 5d.2, then all the better. Below are seven values that will encourage and instil a culture of kindness for a happier, more productive and successful place of work.

If we return to the culture of kindness house, you will have your organisational morals, (the foundations), you have allowed your team/ colleagues and yourself to work through the actions within the book, set your own personal plans, know yourselves a little better and visibly raised your emotional intelligence as individuals. These are your walls.

You have then focused on others. These are the doors and windows. Now the values that you want the company to instil must become something more than just words. They form your roof. The values cannot sit alone, they must have a foundation by which to rest and be secure on. Every roof tile being a tiny action that continues to instil the values into the company.

So how do we do that?

First we need to uncover our values, and those need to match the organisational morals. Why? Because if you have an organisational moral that for example states, 'we own our mistakes', and 'truth' is not one of your values, the house might just fall down. Maybe too dramatic, but we must understand that, when building a house, it is all interconnected.

Then you need to look at whether your organisation's measures and its KPIs (Key Performance Indicators) are in line with its values. This is hugely important. For example, if you choose trust as a key value to the development of the organisation and the wellbeing of your people, then having a KPI target as to how long a person spends on the phone to someone is not a measure that will match the value that you have set.

If you believe that kindness is a key component to making a change in the company and to the world as a whole, then not having any sort of CSR (Corporate Social Responsibility) measure would contradict that idea. The core values set out below are important not only for you to start to cultivate, but also for the company as a whole if you are adopting this culture to make positive change.

After this, you will find a set of KPIs to work with that would complement the suggested organisational morals I laid out in Chapter 4.2. While this is not prescriptive, it should provide a framework as a starting point, think of it as the pre-packed house ready for adaptation.

6.1   Gratitude

gratitude
/ˈɡratɪtjuːd/

noun: gratitude
the quality of being thankful; readiness to show appreciation for, and to return kindness.
"she expressed her gratitude to the committee for their support"
(Oxford Dictionary)

Gratitude defies easy classification. It has been conceptualised as an emotion, an attitude, a moral virtue, a habit, a personality trait, or a coping response. The word gratitude is derived from the Latin root *gratia*, meaning grace, graciousness, or gratefulness. All derivatives from this Latin root *have to do with kindness, generousness, gifts, the beauty of giving and receiving, or getting something for nothing.* (51)

Martin Seligman, a pioneer in the field of Positive Psychology, remarked, *when we take time to notice the things that go right – it means we're getting a lot of little rewards throughout the day.*

Gratitude is so important as it intertwines through the entire concept of this book. To build this value into your culture of kindness 'house' is certainly going to keep you watertight. Gratitude should be promoted throughout your organisation although often, this is not the case.

Thinking about the inspirational leader trait of centredness, this means coming across as mindful, stress-free, calm and composed. It is the trait we all look for in not only leaders, but each other. We have to trust each other to work as a cohesive team. Being grateful for the things you have in your immediate life will promote this trait.

By bringing being grateful into the core of a company, it simply builds a company that is robust, has a team spirit and fosters loyalty.

'Thank you' is one of the simplest belonging cues when it comes to building culture and it is the way to make people feel good and accepted. The impact of thank you is not only that the person will feel good, but they will want to contribute more, because it releases good hormones and therefore helps their overall health.

Research (52) shows that appreciation will result in a 50 percent increase in additional help offered in the workplace. That's no small thing. This additional 50 percent of help comes with a more positive attitude, more motivation and energy, and more willingness to do it all over again the more thanks we receive.

Despite that, a survey conducted by the John Templeton Foundation (53) (which funds an Expanding Gratitude project at UC Berkeley), shows that people are least likely to express gratitude in the workplace, despite feeling a desire to be thanked more often at work themselves.

What stops us thanking others? Is it because we still believe that emotion and business don't sit hand in hand?

A Culture of Kindness

To be grateful means to allow oneself to be placed in the position of a recipient—to feel indebted and aware of one's dependence on others. Gratitude has an obligatory aspect. People are expected to repay kindnesses. Most people experience indebtedness as an unpleasant and aversive psychological state. (54)

Either way society needs to get over whatever is holding us back from giving thanks in the workplace. Gratitude needs to be a central feature of company culture as, like kindness, it is infectious and breeds.

Wong and Brown (55) asked how gratitude affects us mentally and physically. Their study involved assigning students into three groups:

Group one wrote a gratitude letter to another person every week for three weeks.

Group two wrote about their thoughts and feelings about negative experiences.

Group three didn't write anything.

Group one, the gratitude group, reported 'significantly better mental health 4 and 12 weeks after the intervention ended.

The research went onto look at how and why gratitude has this effect. They determined that gratitude does four things:

Gratitude focuses our minds away from the negative and allows thoughts not to circle around events that don't serve us well. Writing a letter appears to shift our attention so that our focus is on emotions that make us feel good. Expressing gratitude even when not giving it to someone, but internalising the gratitude of maybe the things you have in life that you can be thankful for. It was clear that was the exercise that brought joy.

The positive effects of gratitude writing appeared to grow over time. You might not notice the benefit of a daily or weekly practice, but after several weeks and months, you will. Gratitude practice trains the brain to be more in tune with experiencing gratitude, moving those emotional muscles only makes us mentally stronger. Their findings echo research done by Emmons and many others.

Bartlett & DeSteno (56) found there is a positive relationship between kind, helpful behaviour, and feeling grateful. In, *Gratitude and prosocial behaviour: Helping when it costs you*, they discuss this connection in great detail. Throughout three studies they determined:
- gratitude facilitates people to be kinder,
- grateful people help everyone rather than single them out, and
- reminding people who was the individual that they should be kind towards made no difference to their increased kindness to strangers.

There were many ways in which gratitude has been studied and its side effects, but with every act it appeared that there was positive reaction, I have listed a few below.
- Writing a gratitude letter and counting blessings had 'high utility scores and were associated with substantial improvements in optimism'. (57)
- Gratitude buffers people from stress and depression. (58)
- Patients who expressed optimism/gratitude two weeks after an acute coronary event had healthier hearts. (59)
- Gratitude and spiritual well-being are related to positive affect, sleep quality, energy, self-efficacy, and lower cellular inflammation. (Just as kindness is!) (60)
- Gratitude may enhance peace of mind, reduce rumination, and have a negative effect on depressive symptoms. (61)

The studies which did not find any significant impact of gratitude did not take place in the work environment, so do not directly reflect the discussion in this section.

With gratitude, like motivation, dopamine is released into the body that makes us feel good. Our brains recognise this and once we are in the cycle of gratitude, we are more likely to get (beneficially) addicted to it as a way of life.

Kira M. Newman, editor of the Greater Good magazine for Berkley UC highlights that *researchers define appreciation as the act of acknowledging the goodness in life—in other words, seeing the positives in events, experiences, or other people (like our colleagues). Gratitude goes a step further: It recognises how the positive things in our lives—like a success at work—are often due to forces outside of ourselves, particularly the efforts of other people. But this kind of thinking can seem countercultural in the realm of hierarchies and promotions, where everyone is trying to get ahead and may be reluctant to acknowledge their reliance on—or express emotions to—their co-workers.*

We tend to think of organisations as transactional places where you're supposed to be 'professional,' says Ryan Fehr, assistant professor of management at the University of Washington, Seattle, whose paper summarises the landscape of gratitude in business. *We may think that it's unprofessional to bring things like forgiveness or gratitude or compassion into the workplace.* (62)

However again, the evidence clearly states that no one wants to be treated like the robot, we are human and need appreciation.

Appreciation is a cornerstone of the culture at Southwest Airlines. One way the company appreciates employees is by paying attention to special events in their personal lives, from kids' graduations to marriages to family illnesses and recognising them with small gestures like flowers and cards.

We're all encountering different obstacles in our life, we're all celebrating different things in our life, says Cheryl Hughey, managing director of culture at Southwest.

Southwest seems to understand what the research says, that appreciating staff is not about getting more productivity but is about being honest with the appreciation so people enjoy coming to work.

[Gratitude is] *going to make your business more profitable, you're going to be more effective, your employees will be more engaged—but if that's the only reason you're doing it, your employees are going to think you're using them,* says Steve Foran, founder of the program Gratitude at Work. *You have to genuinely want the best for your people.*

Gratitude cannot be forced and contrived, for example, the employee of the month award that lacks depth and has lost favour as a way to motivate. A culture of gratitude can only truly happen when it is driven from the bottom up, the most junior people need to decide how they will not only appreciate their colleagues but also themselves. It must be 'encouraged' from the top down, the organisational morals must have something that demonstrates how gratitude will filter through the company. True appreciation can never lie in hollow gestures ticked off a senior executive's to-do list.

Not every way of demonstrating you are grateful will work for each person in your office. They will respond differently to verbal communications of thanks, the same for a note, a shout out in the company newsletter, or a badge to say they have reached a milestone. A team that has worked through this book will all know their core values. When showing gratitude, tuning into those will make huge strides in ensuring it is genuine and considered thanks.

A Culture of Kindness

Gratitude is a form of love, so Gary Chapman's *Five Love Languages* is a great place to find out who you are and what is most important to you when it comes to being appreciated. (63) He cites five levels of what motivates people in love:

Words of affirmation
Quality time
Receiving gifts
Acts of service
Physical touch

While the idea is about love it is true of all matters of the heart and what drives us. I recommend you go to the website (5lovelanguages.com) and there you can do the test to find out what is most important to you. Obviously, someone who values physical touch, would want to shake someone's hand or pat them on the back. This will guide you on appropriate ways to show gratitude to your colleagues and team.

Gratitude has an important part to play in the theory of positive psychology and through the research, gratitude is strongly and consistently associated with greater happiness. Gratitude helps people feel more positive emotions, relish good experiences, improve their health, deal with adversity, and build strong relationships.

Martin Seligman (64) tested the impact of various positive psychology interventions on 411 people, each compared with a control assignment of writing about early memories. When their week's assignment was to write and personally deliver a letter of gratitude to someone who had never been properly thanked for his or her kindness, those people who wrote the letters immediately exhibited a huge increase in happiness scores. This impact was greater than that from any other positive psychology intervention, with benefits lasting for a month.

The research is extensive not only in the theory of positive psychology but across many theories. The key is to battle against the norms that a work environment gives you and do it anyway. Get addicted to gratitude.

HOW?

Of course, it could be as simple as saying thank you. However, to really bring it into the core of a company you must instil practices that make this part of the essence, that is, not necessarily even named or that are seen as a chore.

I have developed a few ideas that you can use for your individual work on gratitude or within your company.

1. In-house letters and card box for employees to send each other notes of gratitude.
2. A blackboard of gratitude that gets filled up each day with images and notes.
3. Birthdays are always celebrated.
4. Rituals are developed for when new clients come on board.
5. All new recruits are given a personal gratitude journal to record their own gratitude.
6. Family day events or similar.
7. Social events.
8. Think about how you can drive being grateful in your day-to-day practices such as your meetings.

6.2   Trust

trust
/trʌst/

noun
noun: trust

1.
firm belief in the reliability, truth, or ability of someone or something. 'relations have to be built on trust'
2 synonyms: confidence, belief, faith, freedom from suspicion/doubt, sureness, certainty, certitude, assurance, conviction, credence, reliance 'a relationship built on mutual trust and respect'
(Oxford Dictionary)

Building trust increases employee engagement. Employee engagement makes you more productive. More productivity gives you profitability and allows the company to grow or exist.

When I have interviewed CEOs, trust is without question the thing that they will class most often as a key to their success. They strive to be trusted, to build trust and for their teams to feel trusted.

Sally Waterston with her colleagues, had built a thriving business on exactly this, so she had much to say on the topic, including:
Be truthful. If you make a mistake own up.

Jackie Scully of Think publishing says the same. The example she gives is one of an employee who she knows works best on creative projects at home. Asking them to stay in the office to complete tasks just means the work takes longer to deliver and is often a lot less creative. The experience is also more stressful for the individual. She believes you must trust your people and give them space to breathe. To create in surroundings where they feel inspired to do great work, not just for the company but for themselves too.

Sally Waterston also says this, *We* (She refers here to the 'We' as the general human condition) *presume everyone is bad before we say everyone is good. Don't punish everyone for one person not pulling their weight. Setting up a sign in and sign out because of one person does not build trust. If you think people won't be trustworthy, then why would they be trustworthy?*
If people are not performing there is usually a back story and you need to explore and understand what that is before you take action.

Sean Tompkins says:

...I think what we are experiencing and have been experiencing is a complete implosion of trust and I think we would link that with kindness. Ultimately, how do you create the conditions of trust and I think kindness, openness, transparency will help people build trust. I would say every piece of research I have seen has shown a continued erosion and implosion

A Culture of Kindness

in trust in almost everything from CEOs, to brands, trust in politicians, to trust in education, leadership and I think it is a real challenge as to how we rebuild trust, and I think leaders have a really big part to play in that. Kindness has a large part to play in the culture of trust.

Tom Levitt, writer and Consultant, Sector 4 Focus, advises that, in his view, a company is successful if it TRIES:
Transparent
Responsible
Inclusive
Ethical
Sustainable

If you adopt those values then trust will come. Trust is not just a relationship with customers but also many stakeholders and particularly employees. If employees have a sense of purpose and mission then research says that they stay, are more loyal and more productive. There is a crisis of productivity in UK industry today and a lot of it is because the sense of mission and purpose is missing from what a lot of businesses do and how they are run.

The hard facts on this show in the PWC 2016 Global CEO survey which revealed that 50 percent of CEOs worldwide consider lack of trust to be a major threat to their organisational growth. (65)

Paul J. Zak, Harvard researcher, Founding Director of the Center for Neuroeconomics Studies and Professor of Economics, Psychology and Management at Claremont Graduate University, and author of *The Trust Factor: The Science of Creating High Performing Companies* has invested decades researching the neurological connection between trust, leadership, and organisational performance. Over his two decades of research, Zak discovered that *compared with people at low-trust companies, people at high-trust companies report 74% less stress, 106% more energy at work,*

50% higher productivity, 13% fewer sick days, 76% more engagement, 29% more satisfaction with their lives, and 40% less burnout.

Like kindness, he found that 'trust' releases oxytocin and the production of this good hormone is the secret to building strong, committed teams. Just before we get to how to do that, allow me to share some more trust stories and evidence to support the activities I suggest in this book.

Tony Blair, while in office, wrote a paper with a stated aim of, *This Government is pledged to clean up and modernise politics. We want a new relationship between Government and citizens, based on openness and trust.* (66)

In the same document the foreword and commitment from the economic secretary to the treasury, Helen Liddell MP said, *Public confidence in official statistics has for too long been clouded by concerns about their integrity. The Government is committed to changing this. Official statistics are used by people to judge whether Government is delivering on its promises, and they inform decisions that affect everybody daily lives. To fulfil these roles well, official statistics must above all be trustworthy and be seen to be trustworthy.*

This was written in 1998 and the full paper if you are interested is called, *Statistics: a matter of trust.*

Interestingly, 20 years on, some of the things they had hoped to implement have been. Trust in statistics appears to rise year-on-year in the past three years according to NatCen. (67) Change takes time, needing consistent and systematic actions towards the goal. Trust is much the same, you must be consistent.

However, interestingly the 2017 Ipsos MORI Veracity Index reveals that once again politicians sit at the bottom of trusted professions. (68) The year that this survey was completed it had come to light that within Westminster there had been sexual harassment claims. This interestingly did not move the trust levels much (approximately two percent but increased) from the previous year, implying that the trust is as low as it could go. This would suggest that, when we know the truth, we trust more for the future. A simple rule but one that as humans we find hard to deliver on.

As an aside, the caring professions (nurses, doctors, police) are the most trusted. Trust comes from authenticity. For those the world sees a group of people who seek no awards, no limelight. They train to do a job that has little financial reward and simply supports the human population, and win trust in return. Every company or group should have the desire to gain this trust and below we will consider how that happens.

The findings of the report are summarised below. You will see that those who appear to have a financial motivation appear to be trusted the least.

The Ipsos MORI Veracity Index is the longest-running poll on trust in professions in Britain, having been asked consistently since 1983. The 2017 edition reveals the esteem the British public holds for a variety of professions, with some fresh additions in the form of weather forecasters and professional footballers. Key headlines include:
-Nurses remain the most trusted profession in Britain. Ninety-four percent trust them to tell the truth, just ahead of doctors (91 percent).
-Government ministers and politicians are again the least trusted; 19 percent trust ministers and 17 percent trust politicians more generally.

In a follow-up wave conducted after numerous sexual harassment cases in Parliament came to light, trust was at 22 percent and 20 percent - not significantly different to the scores beforehand.

Three quarters trust weather forecasters to tell the truth (76 percent), making them the seventh-most trusted profession.

Trust in the police is at its highest recorded level. At 74 percent, trust has risen by 13 percentage points since 1983.

Trust in professors has risen strongly since 2011, when this profession was last included. Eighty-five percent trust these academics to tell the truth, up from 74 percent six years ago.

Faith in priests is now 20 points lower than in 1983, when they were the most trusted profession. This year two-thirds (65 percent) trust them to tell the truth, their lowest recorded level.

Trust in scientists has equalled the highest recorded level – 83 percent now trust them to tell the truth, the joint-highest recorded score (it was previously this high in 2014). The proportion trusting scientists has risen 20 percentage points since 1997.

Professional footballers are trusted by just a quarter of the public (26 percent), putting them on a par with estate agents (27 percent).

Trust in journalists, while low, is also at a record high. Twenty-seven percent of the public trust them to tell the truth, the highest score since the survey began.

Overall, this year's trust league table looks similar to 2016, with nurses and doctors at the head and politicians and Government ministers at the bottom, below journalists, estate agents and professional footballers.

There is an interesting correlation between how much the people of a country have trust for others, and how that affects the GDP of the country. Arrow (69) says that, *Virtually every commercial transaction has within itself an element of trust, certainly any transaction conducted over a period of time*. It's no coincidence I am sure that the countries that sit high on the trust's vs. GDP scale are also those which are the most giving such as Australia and New Zealand.

As it can be seen from the research, there is a very strong positive relationship with those people whose work is not motivated by money and how much they are trusted. We recognise that, when people are not motivated by money, their motivations are more likely good and we can more easily trust them even when we don't know them. People who have trust are more likely to become entrepreneurs. Trust is about empowering people. If that sounds daunting, the actions in this book are certainly for you.

When asked which of the institutions that Edelman (70) studied was the most broken, 44 percent of us chose government, compared with just 8 percent for media, 4 percent for business and 4 percent for NGOs.

While this is all very depressing regarding our political system, we must accept that this has not changed in thousands of years even though the country has evolved and completely outgrown this old-fashioned way of managing national security. We do however have control of our own environments and companies. One thing you have to be prepared to do is change. If your 1,000-strong company is not built on trust, and the culture is becoming toxic, you still have the power to make that change. It does not matter what is going on externally in the world, politically or otherwise.

How do we start to make that change?

First, **Care**! Care about your people. Who exactly it is you are taking care of? Johnson and Johnson famously had a disaster with Tramadol that had a negative effect on their customers. Their mission statement included a line about them caring about every single man, woman and child that they served in making sure they deliver something that will help them. They made the decision to bring every single tramadol bottle off the shelves. It cost them millions. They were not afraid to say, we don't know, we made a mistake, we will find a way to remedy it. Now that brand has grown year on year.

Own the mistake. Johnson and Johnson accepted the mistake and their response cost them millions, but it put people first over money. Kept to their core value. They told the truth and took action that was only of benefit to the people over the company. It has meant that the company is now more profitable.

Talk in the language everyone understands. Corporations will often use a language all of their own. This might feel great but does not entice new employees, or new customers. Big explanations no longer work. A dear line manager of mine once told me if you can't fit it onto an A4 sheet then don't pitch it to me.

People need to believe facts. There is a growing confidence in the UK at the moment in statistics but that may not be the same for every country or every organisation. State how you came by the evidence, what it aims to achieve and what you plan to do with it. Wages and scales are a great example of building trust that every person doing the same job is on the same salary.

Build followers. Every social media group now has followers, made up of people who believe in your brand, your product or you. This comes from being honest and trustworthy.

Thank you. Giving out a public recognition to a person or group for a great job immediately is important. For example: Your small sales team stayed up late all week putting the tender together for a new project, they have poured their hearts into the bid. You will hear if the company made it through to the next stage in a month. It might be easy to pass by the team and say well done, you might think it is better to say well done when the results come in.

However, what you should be thinking is that you want to thank them that very moment in front of all the office. To gather everyone around and praise the hard work and commitment. It was a tight deadline and whatever happens, if we make it through to next round or not, we can say we put our hearts into it. I have never in my career had that happen, but I have seen it happen in some of the greatest businesses that we know. As I have said be grateful, say thank you, do it from the heart with meaning and you will I guarantee build trust in your organisation. If you are unable to thank your staff, please seek out coaching as this is not an issue with your staff but something you need to work on to be a great leader.

SMART.   SMART (Specific, Measurable, Attainable, Realistic and Time sensitive) is probably one of the most common ways to set goals. In truth, how many people use that when they are assigning an activity to their staff?

So, you have a new project to complete and you have to give out some of that work. People want to be given these challenges and to problem solve, this releases all the good hormones when they get to deliver. However, if you have not checked that the goals you have given out are SMART, then they are usually not achievable and will cause distrust that can and will eat away at the company.

Trusting people and not needing to control everything is an art. It takes work on building the walls to the house, and high levels of self-awareness. However, you will see strong change in productivity if you can make it happen.

Trust takes time to build. Phil Smith, Chairman at IQE, Prev. CEO of Cisco, talked about a situation where they had had a particularly poor employee engagement measurement score (while at Cisco). Phil had been concerned and had set about generating ideas on how to improve it based on the feedback. He then conducted a roadshow to share what would happen, made a plan for a great overall workplace engagement score and, when they redid the survey after all this, there was no change. However, he said they carried on with the plan anyway not for the statistics but just knowing that it was the right thing to do. When they did re-test a year later and every year subsequently, the results just kept on rising. Have patience and be consistent. Trust is not built on words, it's built on actions.

Environment. As Sally Waterston has also proved with the flexible working approach, which has also been proven in recent surveys, autonomy over work conditions communicates to employees that their leadership trusts them. A Citigroup and LinkedIn survey (71) found that nearly half of employees would forfeit a 20 percent raise for greater control over their work environment. It is proven over and over again, that where people can work in an environment where they are happy they will be more productive.

Communicate a lot. Newsletters and internal comms should always go out before external communications. Why? because it shows you trust people. Share everything on the company's direction. Share hopes and dreams. What is discussed on the agenda of the board meetings. It doesn't happen but it should, if there is nothing to hide from the employees which there never should be, then share and share some more. Communication should be done in original ways because you can make it fun, be creative.

6.3   Integrity

integrity
/ɪnˈtɛgrɪti/
noun
1.
the quality of being honest and having strong moral principles.
'a gentleman of complete integrity'
'I never doubted his integrity'

honesty, uprightness, probity, rectitude, honour, honourableness, upstandingness, good character, principle(s), ethics, morals, fairness, scrupulousness, sincerity, truthfulness, trustworthiness

'Integrity is the practice of being honest and showing a consistent and uncompromising adherence to strong moral and ethical principles and values. In ethics, integrity is regarded as the honesty and truthfulness or accuracy of one's actions. Integrity can stand in opposition to hypocrisy, in that judging with the standards of integrity involves regarding internal consistency as a virtue, and suggests that parties holding within themselves apparently conflicting values should account for the discrepancy or alter their beliefs. The word integrity evolved from the Latin adjective *integer*, meaning whole or complete. In this context, integrity is the inner sense of wholeness deriving from qualities such as honesty and consistency of character. As such, one may judge that others have integrity to the extent that they act according to the values, beliefs and principles they claim to hold.'   (Wikipedia) (72)

A person who has integrity lives their values in relationships with coworkers, customers, and stakeholders. Honesty and trust are central to integrity. Acting with honour and truthfulness are also basic principles of a person with integrity.

There is something interesting about integrity in someone. It is not just about being honest, but it also about keeping to the morals set, sticking to their word and doing what they have committed to do. It's the simple things of human decency. However there appears to be a shift in integrity in recent times. I may be incorrect and every person I speak to may just be agreeing with me. However, it appears people are so busy in life that even basic responses and communication appears to be hit and miss. In recent times I have had a few people with high integrity be really honest with me, 'Yes, please email me, but keep pestering if I don't return your email as it will have got lost in the sea of emails.'

If we have made ourselves so accessible as individuals, where does the additional time come from as we seek to be more connected than ever before?

People who are lacking integrity tend to be those that are fearful. They do not see the importance of responding to an email or giving a person a response. A commitment to deliver something does not always take priority. People will always use the excuse of being too busy. However, if integrity is high that person learns to say 'No' to all the requests coming in and focusses only on what they know they can deliver and that can often be frightening, it needs an element of confidence to do that. A person with integrity will always respond and it can more than often be no, but they will always respond. 'I think this would be better placed in a different department...', or 'Sorry our customer service is so busy at present you are likely to get a response through calling.' When people don't know the answer, they often freeze and don't respond at all, that goes not only through technological communication but also in person. This though leads nicely onto honesty.

A Culture of Kindness

Honesty can be elusive in the workplace. We have a fear of saying, 'I don't know'. We don't want to say who we truly are as it might not fit with the company. For example, you put on the mask of the finance manager you hope the company wants you to be to get the job, rather than the human that you actually are. Everyone has had a job like that at some point and if you haven't you are very lucky.

Never be afraid to say you've made a mistake. If we fired people for a making a mistake I wouldn't be here.
Sally Waterston

We make mistakes and then in poor company cultures we are too afraid to own those mistakes, to put our hands up. We also don't want to say, 'I don't know', as it's seen as a sign of weakness and lack of knowledge. 'What are they employing you for if you don't know the answer'. So you make something up to compensate. Then you are in a cycle that is not productive for your own development or the project.

Leaders must promote honesty as a way to work.

Susan M Heathfield provides some brilliant examples of integrity in her article. (73) She really lays bare the varieties of integrity but also its overall importance and why it is so integral to building a culture of kindness.

1. The CEO of the company kept the employees up-to-date on the struggles the business was experiencing with clear and frequent communication at team meetings. Employees felt as if they knew exactly what was happening. They were not blindsided by the CEO's request that they all take a 10 percent pay cut so that the company could avoid layoffs or furloughs for the time being. The employees also felt confident in the turnaround plan they were following as they had helped develop it and they trusted their CEO. (So the CEO was honest about the struggle, owned it and said, it's not going so good. This is what we are trying to do,

can you stand by us as we value you? He said all that without really saying it, simply by his open and honest actions.)

2 John was a developer who had taken a path, that was not working out, to optimise the process the code was supposed to create. Rather than patching together a solution that was not optimum, but that would allow him to save his work, he went to his team. He explained the dead ends he had run into and that he thought that they could create problems for the continual development of advanced features for the software product in the future. The team discussed and worked through the problem. John scrapped all of his code and started from scratch with the team's input. His new solution gave the team the ability to expand the product's capabilities easily in the future.

Owning our shortcomings can be hard but is imperative to the success not only of the work but ourselves and our own growth as humans. We are not designed to work alone.

3. Barbara went to the women's restroom and used up the last bit of toilet paper in her stall. Rather than leave the dispenser empty for the next employee, she tracked down the location of the toilet paper and replaced the empty roll. Sure, it took her five minutes, but she didn't leave the next employee in a bind.

Consideration for the consequences of actions on others is brought about by that strongest Emotional Intelligence wall, self-awareness. Raise this and the rest falls into place.

4. Ellen missed a deadline for an important deliverable her team was supposed to have developed. Rather than throwing her team members under the bus, even though they hadn't delivered as promised, she took responsibility for the missed deadline. She addressed the problems with

her team and they put in place safeguards that would keep them from underperforming again.

Team members recognised their contribution to the failure but there were no repercussions because Ellen took responsibility as the team leader. They also recognised that a repeat failure was not allowed.

Ellen was not simply being a martyr for the cause, to gain favour in some way. She put in actions and worked with the team to say, how will this not happen again, how do we all be better next time. The team bonded more because of it, knowing that their loyalty was increased because of this.

5. Two team members were discussing another team member's failure to perform. They talked critically about the individual's lack of skill and imagination. They criticised his follow-through efforts and his production. Paul entered the room in the midst of the gossip and discussion, listened for a minute, and then, interrupted. He asked the two team members if they had discussed their issues with the employee who they were criticising?

The route of all conflict comes through judgement, blame and unproductive criticism. Paul though clearly embodies a culture of kindness ethos and high integrity. He came in and by saying what he did, he conveyed that this is not consistent with the organisational morals, this is not the way we do it.

6. Mary, the HR manager, was approached by an employee who wanted to formally complain that her boss, a senior manager, was bullying her. Mary immediately investigated the situation and discovered that indeed, the manager was acting in ways that could be considered bullying. Other employees had experienced the same behaviour. Several employees had brought to his attention how his actions made them feel (Brave souls). Mary asked the complaining employee how she wanted the situation handled. The employee asked Mary to mediate a conversation because she

was afraid to talk to him on her own. Mary set up a meeting and was able to facilitate the conversation. She also warned the manager that he could not retaliate against the employee. It would be a positive outcome to say that the manager stopped the behaviour. But, unfortunately, he did not. This required the next step in follow up. Mary finally went to his boss, a Senior VP, who intervened—powerfully and immediately. Then, the person's behaviour changed.

This story is an example of employees doing the right things, having professional courage, and demonstrating personal and professional integrity at each step of the journey.

7. A customer asked Mark, a customer service rep, whether a software product would perform certain functions that she needed. These capabilities were the deciding factors in whether she would purchase the product. Mark thought that the software would perform the needed tasks and told her so.

However, he also indicated that he was not positive and that he would talk with the other reps and the developers and get back to her that day with an answer. After talking with the others, he discovered that one capability was missing. He called the customer who decided to purchase the product anyway as she had been unable to find one that did a better job.

It would have been very easy for Mark to say yes, because he believed that to be true. He wasn't totally sure, but sure enough. By checking and being honest he was able to secure a happy customer who will return over and over again as they know that they will get truth.

8. Marsha was responsible for producing a report once a week that was used on Friday by two other departments to plan their workflow for the next week. Knowing that she planned to take advantage of her vacation

time in the near future, Marsha ensured that the report would be produced as needed in her absence.

She completely prepared another employee to create the report. Additionally, she wrote out the appropriate procedures so that the coworker had a guide in her absence. She supervised the trainee for two weeks so that her replacement had a chance to do the actual task. Finally, she touched base with the other two departments to let them know that a rather inexperienced person would be creating their report in case the coworker needed help.

In big ways and small ways, in visible or invisible situations, we all have the opportunity to demonstrate our integrity.

Let's summarise some of the key points:

The great thing is that, by following the actions highlighted throughout this book, you will find that you have quite naturally started to build the foundations for integrity.

First, by looking at your inner self:

Understanding your self-awareness and making a commitment to grow yourself is key to being in a position of confidence. You will therefore have less fear about tackling situations, which will empower you to act with integrity.

Have a sense of your own purpose. This may seem elusive, however, when you have your values your purpose follows quite easily. In the example on p.129, Nick 's core values were family, security and reliability. His mission statement might be:

'My aim is to provide security for my family, not only from a material point of view but also to ensure that I am emotionally available and make sure I always have time for them first. I want to always be seen by them and the people in my life as reliable and constant.'

Why not have a go on Appendix 5 by adding your own mission statement in at the bottom of the page.

Learn to say no. Be ok with saying no and putting in the boundaries of what you can and can't do. It's about having clear goals and working on them not being influenced by all the other shiny things that come into your line of sight.

It is ok not to know. Don't let your ego be bigger than the moment. When you understand what it is to be ok with not knowing, people follow suit around you. It is important that you are willing to seek out the knowledge and share what you find.

Looking at your team and the outer self.

Get people to respond. Making sure your teams are responding to each other and to customers. Ensuring that they have time management in place and clear goals will support them to improve their integrity.

Don't belittle. People will make mistakes, sometimes not perform as they or you might want and when someone is honest to own up to the mistake, the answer is not to be deter that. Instead be thankful for their honesty. Ask them what they think might work to remedy that.

Giving notifications, not giving commands is a brilliant response in stressful situations. What do you know? What don't you know? Questions that end with, has anyone got ideas? Even when you feel you should know, it is a great gift to a team environment to help it grow but also to navigate the problem they are trying to get over the challenge they are facing.

Feedback is one of the most important things we can deliver. It is the thing that leaders dread and can often really just not be very good at. However, if within the culture all the things that did not go right with a project or piece of work is valued, positive change can happen. If everyone asks first, what could I change on this to make it better? What would allow this message to be delivered better? What is missing from this?

The key to building integrity in to allow honesty without judgement, to be honest in what you say you are able to deliver and ultimately do it with kindness.

6.4   Empathy

empathy
/ˈɛmpəθi/
noun

he ability to understand and share the feelings of another.

Synonyms : affinity with, rapport with, understanding of, sensitivity towards, sensibility to, identification with, awareness of, fellowship with, fellow feeling for, like-mindedness, togetherness, closeness to; informal chemistry
"what is really important about learning a language is learning empathy for another culture".

Mother Teresa (1910-1997) told us that empathy has to start with us. She said *Do not wait for leaders; do it alone, person to person.*

On the need for empathy in the workplace:

It has gone beyond a need, people are crying out for it. I think for a long period of time we went through a rise in motivation and being positive all the time and seize the day. It can't come at the expense of validation. People are craving the realness and vulnerability. To be leader you have to vulnerable.

Josh Connolly, Life leadership and performance coach,
Freedom From Within

Research reported in *Scientific American* suggests that our levels of empathy, or the ability to understand the feelings of others, are lower today than 30 years ago. An increase in social isolation is one theory used to explain this finding. Digital communication, social networking, video conferencing and other forms of new media contribute to social isolation and are often blamed for the reduction in empathy. After all, as Simon Kempton has previously highlighted, it's much easier to say negative things about others if you don't have to say it to their face. And if I don't feel like engaging in your problems, I can simply log off, or even 'unfriend' you. It's an easy option.

The trouble is that, when there is no empathy, when we don't work to understand the needs of others, there is a significant loss of trust. If I don't really know what you're thinking and feeling I trust you less, and isolate myself more. This can have major implications for business where trust is essential for successful leadership and partnerships. This is also not just within work but is also with our communities, our own families and society as whole.

(Bear) Grylls said: *In a world that sometimes feels fractured and insular, empathy and kindness are more important than ever. When society is polarised we need to work twice as hard to understand each other and find ways of working together. I believe young people have a right to* develop key skills such as empathy and kindness and we urgently need more adult volunteers to help us do this. (74)

Ben Page, the chief executive of Ipsos Mori, said studies had shown that people born before 1945 and the establishment of the NHS and the welfare state were more empathetic towards the poor than each subsequent generation.

This continued until the [2008] crash, when empathy increased but levels have still not returned to that of the 1980s, he said. *We have become a society less empathetic to the working-age poor.*

Matt Hyde, chief executive of the Scout Association, (74) said: *There is a worrying decline in empathy in the UK. We have a polarised politics and I don't think social media helps. People are retreating into their own friendship circles and not engaging with people different to them.*

When I interviewed Byron Vincent, he shared with me how he thought we could make a culture of kindness.

I had a really interesting meeting with a professor at Berkley University called Jodi Halpern. She's an amazing working class, Brooklyn, Jewish woman in her 60s. The first in her family to go to university and now a senior professor at Berkley. She said an interesting thing that has stuck with me, she said 'the best way to engender empathy is to tell a really good story'. That sentiment really resonated with me. It's informed much of the work I've done since. We can step over homeless people in the street and not think twice about it, but if the dog in our favourite soap opera dies we feel devastated. The reason being that we have a narrative for that dog and we don't have a narrative for the person we've stepped over. So in terms of helping create a culture of kindness I strive to tell stories that engender empathy, stories that encourage, enable and empower people to find their own voice in the hope that we can become a little bit more connected. As you can read, it was a great ending to that podcast.

In the DiSalvo and Keltner interview mentioned in Chapter 1.3, Keltner talks about his research that highlights the importance of teasing that helps empathy grow within children. I found what he said and his research to be important, however I advise anyone looking at teasing as a way to promote connection in a workplace to tread carefully. This must be done with caution and consideration and a high emotional intelligence overall. Keltner: *Teasing is the art of playful provocation, of using our playful voices and bodies to provoke others to avoid inappropriate behaviors.*

Marc Bekoff, a biologist at the University of Colorado, Boulder, has found in some remarkable work with coyotes that they sort out leaders from aggressive types in their rough-and-tumble biting. The coyotes that bite too hard in such provocative play are relegated to low status positions. We likewise accomplish so much with the right kind of teasing.

Teasing (in the right way, which is what most people do) offers so much. It is a way to play and express affection. It is a way of negotiating conflicts at work and in the family. Teasing exchanges teach children how to use their voices in innumerable ways—such is important medium of communication. In teasing, children learn boundaries between harm and play. And children learn empathy in teasing, and how to appreciate others' feelings (for example, in going too far). And in teasing we have fun. All of this benefit is accomplished in this remarkable modality of play.

Brené Brown is very famous for her conversations on the difference between empathy and sympathy. She states that stories are data with a soul, just as Vincent says, the art to building a culture of kindness is in his eyes to tell stories and I am sure Brown agrees. Her research on shame led her to recognise that among other characteristics, empathy was one of the key solutions to eradicating shame but also to how people lived wholeheartedly.

A Culture of Kindness

Brown often quotes nursing scholar Theresa Wiseman's four attributes of empathy:

• To be able to see the world as others see it—this requires putting our stuff aside to see the situation through the eyes of a loved one.

• To be non-judgmental—judgement of another person's situation discounts the experience and is an attempt to protect ourselves from the pain of the situation.

• To understand another person's feelings—we need to be in touch with our personal feelings in order to understand someone else's. This also requires putting aside "us" to focus on our loved one.

• To communicate our understanding of that person's feelings—rather than saying, 'At least...' or 'It could be worse...' try, 'I've been there, and that really hurts,' or (to quote an example from Brown) 'It sounds like you are in a hard place now. Tell me more about it.' (75)

Consider the difference between empathy and sympathy as laid out by Brown. She highlights that empathy fuels connection, while sympathy drives disconnection. Empathy is feeling with people. She describes the picture of someone being stuck in a dark hole. Empathy is when we go down the hole and join them and say, you are not alone. Sympathy is looking in the hole and going, 'Yeah that looks bad, sorry for you.' Empathy does not happen when you try to add the silver lining. 'I feel sad because I don't have a home, but at least you have some food.' 'My grandmother just died...well at least she had a good life'.

It is easy in a work environment where we are led by action to allow other people's feelings to be discarded. However, to build connections and a culture that is kind, we must be able to sit in the moment with someone and really listen to how they feel with no judgement over and over again.

As I have stated previously, we are not the same, we are not meant to be. It does mean that people whose opinions differ from our own should judged, but we need to find a way to accept and be open-minded about the differences.

Psychologists Daniel Goleman and Paul Ekman break down the concept of empathy into the following three categories.

Cognitive empathy is being able to understand how another person feels and what they might be thinking. Having high cognitive empathy makes us better communicators, because it helps us give information in a way that the other person is able to understand. Like speaking the language of that person.

Emotional empathy (also known as affective empathy) means being able to share and understand the feelings of someone else. Some have called it 'your pain in my heart'. This type of empathy helps build emotional connections with others. It's when someone tells you a sad story and you weep with them not because it makes you sad but because you feel their pain.

Compassionate empathy (also known as empathic concern) goes beyond simply understanding others and sharing their feelings: it actually moves us to take action, to help however we can.

To illustrate how these three branches of empathy work together, imagine that a friend has recently lost a close family member. Your natural reaction may be sympathy, a feeling of pity, or sorrow. Sympathy may move you to express condolences or to send a card, and your friend may appreciate these actions.

They say that we work through these stages of empathy, to first understand the person, to then feel what they feel and then eventually to be compelled to take action.

A Culture of Kindness

Empathy can be challenging when we feel so consumed in our own stories, when we can't bear to look at another's sadness or upset. However we need to simply learn to sit in the moment with the person and say, 'I hear you and I am here'.

ACTION

Role play with people when they first start in the company is a great way to develop this. However, first show people good and bad examples of people having a bad day, get people in your company to act it out. Let your new recruits be their partners' person they have gone to and allow them to respond. Allow them to feedback on themselves first and then the partner who is having a bad day. We can and should be teaching what empathy really looks like. Don't expect everyone to know.

Consider how to grow each element of the empathy.

Building cognitive empathy
Consider what you know about the person you are listening to. Communication can often be misinterpreted and instincts can be wrong. Spend time with people testing this ability and make it a strength.

Building emotional empathy
When a person shares with you how they feel about something or when something that is bothering them. It is important to be able to take time to reflect. Once you have a better understanding of how that person might feel you are better able to relate and be present.

A great way to practice this emotional empathy is to ask yourself, when have I felt similar to this person?

Exercising compassionate empathy

A great question to ask yourself when considering the action part of the empathy stage is, What would have helped me in this situation? What would I appreciate right now if I were them? Take yourself back to the 'In their shoes exercise'. Although remember, comparison is not compassionate. No one wants to hear you've had it happen but 1,000 times worse.

6.5   Time

time
/taɪm/

noun
1. the indefinite continued progress of existence and events in the past, present, and future regarded as a whole.
'travel through space and time'
2. a point of time as measured in hours and minutes past midnight or noon.
'the time is 9.30'

verb
1. plan, schedule, or arrange when (something) should happen or be done.
'the first track race is timed for 11.15'

2. measure the time taken by (a process or activity, or a person doing it).
'we were timed and given certificates according to our speed'

Time is the indefinite continued progress of existence and events that occur in an apparently irreversible succession from the past, through the present, to the future. Time is a component quantity of various measurements used to sequence events, to compare the duration of events or the intervals between them, and to quantify rates of change of quantities in material reality or in the conscious experience. Time is often referred to as a fourth dimension, along with three spatial dimensions.
Wikipedia

Who needs you? It is the basis of who we are as human beings. Who needs me today?

Giving people time was undoubtedly the value that was unanimously highlighted among the guests interviewed in season 1 of the *Culture of Kindness* podcast. They said it was essential for ensuring you have the best team around you. Being present and, of course, listening.

Ben Mathes is founder of the social movement, Urban Confessional: a free listening movement. Since he started it in 2012 it has grown to over 80 countries with thousands of volunteers holding simple handwritten signs that say 'Free Listening'. Benjamin does not call this a 'soft skill' as most might consider, he says it's a 'survival skill'. On the podcast he says that, while he recognises it is imperative for us as a race, he understands why we are always learning to listen and therefore to give time is the most important gift we can give.

Being present and allowing time to pass with someone isn't always easy, it is sometimes our own minds that are consumed by our own stories that lets us down. Getting out of that and giving time to others, your team and work colleagues, is what will ultimately build better bonds.

However, what happens when you haven't got any time? You know you are working at your best with your great time management plan, but it's high pressure and deadlines must be met. Time is the one thing that you don't have!

Simon Kempton provides a very real and interesting take on this. He says leadership in the police will differ not just from person to person but also from incident to incident. *When people's lives are in danger I will give an order and expect it to happen as we don't have time for the please and thank you and how I speak with a person. There are other situations however that I should sit down with my team to take the time to get to know them, get to know what motivates them and what is a blocker for them achieving what they want to achieve. So many of their concerns might not be in my control to gift but many of them will. So, it's little things I can do, the little things that I can do to get them, as their line manager, to help them get through the day, the week or the shift. That's so much more important.*

In the police force and any life-and-death role, time is of the essence. We have no time for the niceties when someone's life is in danger. However, time, as he states, is still hugely important when those situations are no longer at the forefront. To sit down and spend time with people. Consciously and deliberately, particularly after the pressure has died down.

Said to much laughter, Russell Brand humorously tells the Sunday Brunch presenters when they say they have run out of time for the interview, *'We haven't run out of time, time continues. It's everywhere, we don't even know what it is do we, let's be honest. It's entropy, it's space'.*

Time in truth is just something that has uniformly been agreed to measure the journey of life and existence. It works so that we can co-exist. While the idea of time on a worldwide scale had been designed long ago, creating and maintaining it in the way we understand it did not happen in the UK until 1847 when GMT (Greenwich Mean Time) was designated. Interestingly, this coincided with the Industrial Revolution. Our growth into consumerism and our desire to trade more globally, I am sure was no coincidence.

However, whether Russell Brand likes it or not, time is now seen as a commodity, which is becoming more precious than gold for some. So much so it is affecting the way we interact. We have moved to a very open society where we can communicate with 80 percent of the world through one method or another in seconds. We can make contact with apparent strangers with ease. That means no-one has time to get back to anyone, we are effectively clogging up time. We have filled our time so efficiently with the things we 'have' to do that we don't have time to see the world around us and who really needs us, including ourselves.

There is a Chinese saying that says, 'If you want happiness for an hour, take a nap, if you want happiness for a day, go fishing. If you want happiness for a year, inherit a fortune. If you want happiness for a lifetime, help someone.' The Stoics also believed that life is about what you can do for others. However, the world was very different then, now everyone is so accessible we have to really home in on our areas of importance, those people we play roles for (as you will have completed in Appendix 5) and decide which of them might need you today. Scientific research (76) tells us that giving is an amazing pathway to personal growth and long-term happiness.

As a leader being direct about looking at who needs your support and what you can do with your own time to do that will grow your team in the healthiest and most efficient way.

A Culture of Kindness

ACTION

Find a way to get back to people who email you. Whether that is an out of office saying you receive up to 1,000 emails a day, and therefore it's unlikely you'll respond, but if it's urgent, to call the main office and leave details.

If you are sending more than two emails back and forth, find a better way to communicate. Pick up the phone or set up an action tracker if it's a constant communication update on a project.

Use your diary like your bible to make sure the people who need you are given the time they need. That can include your family. Did you do date night? Did you get too busy to spend time on the floor playing with your children? Block it out, take the time.

Ask yourself at the beginning of each day, Who needs me today? But also note that the answer will include, you.

6.6   Connection

connection
/kəˈnɛkʃ(ə)n/

noun
noun: connection; plural noun: connections; noun: connexion; plural noun: connexions
1. a relationship in which a person or thing is linked or associated with something else.
'the connections between social attitudes and productivity'

the action of linking one thing with another.
'connection to the Internet'

'ensure that all connections between the wires are properly made'
a link between two telephones.
an arrangement or opportunity for catching a connecting train, bus, aircraft, etc.
people with whom one has social or professional contact or to whom one is related, especially those with influence and able to offer one help.
'he had connections in the music industry'

synonyms:contact, friend, acquaintance, ally, colleague, associate, sponsor

We are creatures that crave connection and connection comes with kindness. You have to be kind enough to allow people into your space so you can hold that space. So I guess that's what real kindness is for me. Going beyond the giving that we do for each other, real kindness is opening the gateway to your space and allowing someone to come in and to share one another in all your glory.

Josh Connolly, Life leadership and performance coach,
Freedom From Within

Relationships are all about finding connections, building trust and showing appreciation to other people. There is no better way to do this than to focus on another person's character strengths and express yours. There is a good reason to make this a priority. Research (77) indicates that one of the most powerful pathways to happiness is creating and maintaining positive relationships.

The values held by you, your people and your organisation have to be the focus for all decisions in normal or tough times. It should govern behaviours.

Your team must find a way to identify where they currently are, and where they want to go. If you want a team to perform at their best, them deciding the route is key to getting value for them and the company as a whole. They will in turn move as one when trauma hits, nor will they allow unkindness into their team. They will adapt to the needs of the business, customers and environment for the greater good. Connections will happen.

Every human has a value and a contribution in some form. This will only shine through following consistent and tiny actions. For example, when people are kind, and a person feels supported, and called upon for the contributions they can offer. When a person feels spoken to honestly

A Culture of Kindness

and with kindness, they feel valued, part of something and not excluded. I could go on. All of these tiny actions must be carried out every day with colleagues and employees to build the connections that make for a great working environment.

In *The Culture Code* by Daniel Coyle, (7) there is a wonderful story about how he learned to build belonging. Coyle discusses one piece of his research, in which a writer called Neil Payne went about finding out who was the best national basketball association coach. He took all the information on the players and the historical games won and the team overall. He used the data to predict through an algorithm which should or shouldn't have won according to the predictive patterns. All the information on all the teams seemed to match what was expected except for the coach Greg Popovitch, he was the coach for the San Antonio spurs. His team had, according to the statistics won 117 games more than they should have. It was even more than double the next team.

The summary was interesting. Several key things made the difference. The team puts the interests of the team above each player's own interests on the court, and this is believed to be the behaviour that sets them apart from the rest.

Popovitch is old school, meaning that he values discipline and he has a temper. So how does he achieve what he does when we know that those behaviours are not in line with getting the best from a team? Notably, he couples his strict approach with other behaviours that are stronger. For example, he laughs a lot, has physical contact, has learnt to speak different languages in line with his team, and even after the team loses he is known to focus on 'filling their cup'. He keeps connection with them all no matter what happens, when they lose and when they win, he is their constant support.

'He will tell you the truth and then love you to death'. This right here is the theory of unconditional love, something that sets him above the rest. It is rare because it involves us being vulnerable and as previously discussed we know it to be one thing that many struggle with. Popovitch would spend time with the players being involved in their lives not talking about basketball. He wanted to be unselfish and build a high-trust relationship, to get to know them, to understand if that person can take his coaching style; he wants them to know either way.

Rather than follow the crowd, he carved out a way to manage his team on his own terms and it paid off. He will often be found sharing with his team not just things about basketball but videos or knowledge that is interesting or inspiring for life in general. He asks a lot of questions that are personal and direct, focussing on the big picture. What do you think? What would you do? Something that I have raised in previous chapters. Connection is key to him. 'Hug 'em and hold 'em' is what has been said about his approach. He avoids all technology and communicates in person, making sure they eat together as much as they play a game.

Popovich is an example of great leadership and a case study on how to build connection. He does not sit in an ivory tower, nor belittle people when things go wrong. He stands strong by his expectations, but understands his team and knows they are all human trying their best.

Coyle talks about 'belonging cues' in his book and Popovich clearly demonstrates them. He will be truthful even when it's uncomfortable, he will give the tough feedback. But then he will also tell the person, 'you are part of this team, we have high standards, I believe you can reach those standards.' His physical cues are that he is always up close and personal, not hiding behind technology. All this behaviour and attention is focused on the team and what he is saying by doing that is very simply, 'I care'. His frequent performance feedback constantly translates to – We have high standards. By holding larger conversations not on the subject they are working on but on politics, food, family, life etc, he is saying to his team that life is bigger than just this.

A Culture of Kindness

What appears evident is that, in giving the uncomfortable truth and telling them where we need to be, he builds connection. However, that does involve courage which we will discuss subsequently.

When you lose, or you don't win the tender, or the launch didn't go as planned, the natural reaction is to retreat and take time. However, a leader will stay close to the team. Popovich did exactly that on a big loss they had. The after-game dinner was planned and he made sure he got there before everyone else, set up the table just right and then greeted them all individually in a personal and unique way. He made sure they always ate together, he didn't talk about the loss, he just chose to be present and give time.

Emotional connections inside and outside of the company appear to be the top employee requirement and in turn make a successful business. If you set things up right and encourage the right organisational morals, (see Chapter 4.2) connection will happen. Setting the foundations, the rules for how we behave is key to making those connections positive.

Allowing people to connect with others is also key to kindness and happiness in life. However, this must be done with love, not for personal gain. When it's not genuine, the connections will be worse than having nothing at all. The way we work and live affects the way we connect to those around us. The environment is crucial and showing others that it matters helps connection.

Environment is hugely important, even down to the locations of desks in relation to each other, and the way we group departments and place people to in relation to each other. Think flow of information. I cannot tell you the amount of people that I have spoken to that leave businesses because senior managers would not understand the need to move departments onto the same floor or area. People are frustrated when they don't have an opportunity to easily connect with the people they need to progress a project effectively. Communication is obviously key to ensuring you are connecting through those 'belonging cues'. You cannot do this if the location of people is not aligned. People also need space, times and areas in which to connect. Whether your organisation is one whose staff are remote or office workers, it is your role to make these places/ opportunities available.

Eye- and physical contact is the age-old indicator of belonging, and we need to remember that, while the world has moved on, our brains are still wired with elements of our basic instincts. We are far more likely to interact with people who are physically closer even using technology. The closer you are, the more efficient your team will be.

Are you making your people feel safe? Seriously, it's a hugely important question to be asking yourself. We do this for children, we understand that they need this to fully learn things in life. Children who feel unsafe will not learn or react in predicable ways, they will act out. Adults are the same, if we do not make the people in our team or life feel safe they will not learn and their behaviours will be turbulent. We all want to feel safe to have true connections.

A Culture of Kindness

ACTION

Ask yourself, 'What can I do differently to build connections?'

Share daily vulnerability. Be real about who you are, and be ok with making mistakes. It takes time to build connections and a successful culture.

So, ask your team and the people around you for feedback on the following questions. Don't do it once, do it often and gain feedback that you then convert to practical solutions.

What should I continue doing?

What should I do more often?

What can I do to make you more effective?

The rules for connection are simple, be real and be you. These are quick and easy rules for people to follow that will bring clarity, communication and connection at times when they are most needed.

A Culture of Kindness

6.7   Courage

courage
/'kʌrɪdʒ/

noun
noun: courage

the ability to do something that frightens one; bravery.
　'she called on all her courage to face the ordeal'
strength in the face of pain or grief.
　'he fought his illness with great courage'
　synonyms:　　bravery, braveness, courageousness, pluck, pluckiness, valour,
fearlessness,　　　　　　　　intrepidity, intrepidness, nerve, daring, audacity,
boldness; More
　antonyms:　　cowardice, timidity

I have closed with this section on courage for a good reason. It is fundamentally the biggest blocker if you don't have it, for any progress in life.

The opposite of courage according to any good thesaurus is fear, timidity or cowardice. We are going to focus on the first two in this section. There is a wonderful saying, 'the opposite to courage is not cowardice it is conformity'. We know that conformity when it comes to a process is a good way to function within a business. However, conformity when it comes to creativity, when making positive change and development, is perhaps less good. We have to be brave in breaking the routine and the norms to really move things forward.

Nigel Prideaux, Communications Director for Aviva, whom I interviewed, had some great things to say on kindness, namely this on having frank conversations:

Sometimes it's about having the tough conversations upfront and openly with them. Of course it's about celebrating success and really motivating people but there is a harder kind of success as well because if for example there is underperformance in a team the kinder thing is to help that person think about how they can increase their performance because it will be better for the individual and it'll be better for the team.

Those tough and honest conversations that I introduced in the section on honesty, are not easy to have, but as a leader we avoid them as the person may be tricky to deal with. We don't want to end up in HR and have the headache of them retaliating about a conversation you have had. It's due to the fear of what might happen. Although you need to draw upon courage to change that, allowing that poor performance will only lead their actions to affect the rest of the team as Prideaux points out. So, how do we draw upon our courage up to tackle those conversations that we may prefer to leave?

Fear is the reason. It is hardwired into our brains, which as previously discussed, was great when we were fighting off sabre tooth tigers. Now we need it much less, although it remains important in many ways to prevent us entering dangerous situations without a sense of caution.

Fear comes from several places, and some is learnt through negative experiences. We may have been attacked in a dark place and then be afraid of the dark. Some are passed on, such as if your mother was frightened of water and showed that she was, then you too are likely to be afraid of water and swimming. And then there is the instinctive fear that we have for something that could cause us pain for example, like a snake.

The ability to fear can keep us alive but it can also be a curse. As humans we are able to imagine what might happen, and we do this a lot. We imagine all the possible outcomes and mostly they are bad. This can escalate into anxiety. Also when we are primed for fear, let's say when you watch a scary movie, when someone walks into the room you'll likely jump. At work it is no different. If we feel our boss is not telling us something and then calls us into a meeting, we are already fearful before it starts.

Fear is a blocker for many people trying to live the life they desire. They conform and behave in ways society expects them to, although this may not actually be bringing them contentment. There is the fear of all the things that could go wrong, what people will think, and the idea of being ostracised and living alone forever. Although in reality the things we think will happen usually don't, and if they do, it's not usually a bad thing in the end.

Courage can grow, once you have achieved one thing you feel brave enough to try the next thing. You know this is true for you, so you know this is true of your team. If you can encourage them to try something new, to take on a new challenge with support, they will be willing to try it again.

Department heads have the power to implement change. Whether your team is 2 or 200, you have the power to make change that can filter out into the wider organisation. Courage is a life gift whose value will never be forgotten by your team. You will be an organisation that becomes a leader in your industry. Of course, things won't always work out perfectly, but that's the point of courage. You dust yourself off and have the courage to do something new or try again. Having the courage to start to make that change, be original, be creative, saying yes before you say no, will change your life and those that you work with, for and on behalf of.

So how do we promote courage in ourselves and our teams which will in turn reduce fear?

Encourage – Encourage your team to think outside the parameters and norms of your industry. No idea is ever discarded, everyone is written down in a brainstorm. Remember in Chapter 5b.5 about the idea of only providing positive feedback on it? That applies here. It encourages people to be brave with sharing their ideas.

Avoid procrastination – This can be a killer. Spend too much time considering a situation or action, and it never gets done. Mel Robbins famously talks about the five-second rule, count five and then do it. Avoidance comes at the price of the fear building up, it's how anxiety is formed and phobias adopted.

Get it booked – Getting things booked in with others will usually help. Summoning the courage to do something, to call that person who might say no. If you don't call at all they certainly are saying no.

Bring a friend – Getting your team to work with each other on something that someone feels uneasy about will help them to have courage. Someone might have to give a presentation and they look like a rabbit in the headlights. Get a colleague who is a great mentor to work with them on it.

Visualisation – Thinking about the feeling when you've managed to achieve it or you have taken the action that was so fear inducing, is just the best. Knowing that you will be able to say, well I did it, will only promote more courage to keep doing things that push you out of your comfort zone.

Be uncomfortable – Be out of your comfort zone regularly. It can be a performance measurement to work with on yourself and your team. Ask what has made you uncomfortable this month?

Serve others – Do things for people, be kind, follow the Culture of Kindness ethos and you will give courage to your team and yourself.

7. Conclusion

I have never met a person who says, 'I want a boss who is unkind. Someone who really doesn't care about me and certainly never shows me any gratitude, I don't trust and never listens to me'. However, what tends to happen is we don't share what we do actually want from a working relationship. We accept whatever comes to us. This lack of boundaries allows many working relationships to break down quickly. However, we are entering a new dawn. One in which our next generations will not tolerate the behaviours that our older generations once would. As a modern leader it is your place to set that precedence; to give governance on what a great working environment represents.

If you have gotten this far and you have thought, 'My company won't go for this' or 'This won't make a difference.' Then I ask you to understand that there are many things that are going on in the world at any one time that are unsettling and we often think we have no power to change them. We can struggle to understand why politicians take the actions that they do. Why some people are treated differently in the world. However, what I hope this book allows you to consider is that you have the power to make a change to your immediate surroundings, to the people you work with and to improve their well-being. If everyone who reads this does that, we all have a chance to make lasting and positive change to workplaces and ultimately our wider communities.

In the words of Barack Obama aptly in his farewell address,

Change only happens when ordinary people get involved, get engaged and come together to demand it. I am asking you to believe. Not in my ability to bring about change – but in yours.

A Culture of Kindness

7.1   Measurement

We measure everything and while this is great to understand progress, sometime this measurement can in fact be counterproductive. Performance Management of individuals can be one of those times. The best companies' performance management systems tend to place an emphasis on evidence-based development of skills and relationships.

The basis of getting a sturdy house will always be from your people. Taking care of the family if you like. So, measuring them on their involvement and ensuring they are taking care of themselves will not only produce a happier workforce but will also make your team or family more loyal and productive as a consequence.

I have provided you with a template that you can use in this chapter, it is based on the performance measurement system of the whole person. However, it is also based on the ideas of this book and developing it around a culture of kindness. You don't need to use the entire sequence of questions, you can cherry pick for each individual. However, the main point here is you should be asking questions. Questions are the key to nurturing and getting the best from people. When you understand how to care for the person you then understand how to get the best for them and the work that they do. Get them thinking for themselves about what they can do, not simply tell them or test them. If they haven't got answers to your questions because they have never considered it, that's great; what positive action are they going to take to improve that area.

Allow the person to be the person, to grow into a place that is comfortable not that fits into a box we produce for them.

Appendices
Appendix 1-4

Appendix 1: MINDFULNESS PROGRAM

https://www.actonsocialanxiety.com/pdf/magt_for_SAD_2nd_ed.pdf

Appendix 2: PROFILING TESTS TO COMPLETE

https://www.nahlasummers.com/eq-quiz
https://www.123test.com/disc-personality-test/
https://www.123test.com/career-test/
https://engaging.works/ew/profile/sample
https://sapa-project.org

Expand on these as you feel appropriate.

Appendix 3: USEFUL CONTACTS AND REFERENCES

Engaging work – www.Engaging.works
Synergy – www.synergyheart2heart.team
Six Seconds - https://www.6seconds.org

Appendix 4 : EMOTIONAL WHEEL

A downloadable copy of this is available at www.nahlasummers.com

Appendix 5: WHO AM I?

Values	
1	
2	
3	
4	
5	
Strengths	
Weak points	
Personal Mission Statement	

A Culture of Kindness

ROLES

This is where you will state your personal roles and what that means to you. I have given one example, however more roles could include: Mother, Father, Sister, Brother, Daughter, Son, Club member, Group member, Speaker, Role model, Carer, Aunt, Uncle, Godparent, Religious position, Volunteer position, Line Manager, Specialist, Colleague and so on. Your roles will be unique to you but the more you delve into your roles the more you will gain from the exercise.

Role	Description
Father	Carer, supporter, need to be care free, install the rules, teacher, support, carer and so on.

Appendix 6: DIARY OF EMOTIONS

Use this daily for 30 days, so take copies as necessary or download a template from www.nahlasummers.com

Day	
Time	
Emotion felt	
Physical reaction	
Trigger	
Other emotions I felt today (using the emotional wheel)	

Appendix 7: VALUES LIST

Acceptance	Potential
Accomplishment	Power
Accountability	Innovation
Accuracy	Inquisitive
Achievement	Insightful
Adaptability	Inspiring
Alertness	Integrity
Altruism	Intelligence
Ambition	Intensity
Amusement	Intuitive
Assertiveness	Irreverent
Attentive	Joy
Awareness	Justice
Balance	Kindness
Beauty	Knowledge
Boldness	Lawful
Bravery	Leadership
Brilliance	Learning
Calm	Liberty
Candour	Logic
Capable	Love
Careful	Loyalty
Certainty	Mastery
Challenge	Maturity
Charity	Meaning
Cleanliness	Moderation
Clear	Motivation
Clever	Openness
Comfort	Optimism
Commitment	Order

Common sense
Communication
Community
Compassion
Competence
Concentration
Confidence
Connection
Consciousness
Consistency
Contentment
Contribution
Control
Conviction
Cooperation
Courage
Courtesy
Creation
Creativity
Credibility
Curiosity
Decisive
Decisiveness
Dedication
Dependability
Determination
Development
Devotion
Dignity
Discipline
Discovery
Drive

Patience
Peace
Performance
Persistence
Present
Productivity
Professionalism
Prosperity
Purpose
Quality
Realistic
Reason
Recognition
Recreation
Reflective
Respect
Responsibility
Restraint
Results-oriented
Reverence
Rigor
Risk
Satisfaction
Security
Self-reliance
Selfless
Sensitivity
Serenity
Service
Organization
Originality
Passion

A Culture of Kindness

Effectiveness	Sharing
Efficiency	Significance
Empathy	Silence
Empower	Simplicity
Endurance	Sincerity
Energy	Skill
Enjoyment	Skillfulness
Enthusiasm	Smart
Equality	Solitude
Ethical	Spirit
Excellence	Spirituality
Experience	Spontaneous
Exploration	Stability
Expressive	Status
Fairness	Stewardship
Family	Strength
Famous	Structure
Fearless	Success
Feelings	Support
Ferocious	Surprise
Fidelity	Sustainability
Focus	Talent
Foresight	Teamwork
Fortitude	Temperance
Freedom	Thankful
Friendship	Thorough
Fun	Thoughtful
Generosity	Timeliness
Genius	Tolerance
Giving	Toughness
Goodness	Traditional
Grace	Tranquillity

Gratitude	
Greatness	Transparency
Growth	Trust
Happiness	Trustworthy
Hard work	Truth
Harmony	Understanding
Health	Unity
Honesty	Welcoming
Honour	Winning
Hope	Wisdom
Humility	Wonder
Imagination	Valour
Improvement	Victory
Independence	Vigour
Individuality	Vision
Playfulness	Vitality
Poise Uniqueness	Wealth

A Culture of Kindness

Appendix 8: DREAMS PAGE

As you make your way through the book I hope you will use this page to dream not only your own dreams, as part of the big goal development but also start to take ideas on how you can develop your own Culture of Kindness.

Appendix 9: Performance Criteria Proforma

This is available in a landscape printable version at
www.nahlasummers.com in the free downloads section.

Performance Criteria Guideline

Area	Criteria	Discussion points	Actions if any.
General	How are you? What is going on right now for you? Things you are enjoying? Challenges in life?		
	Do you have plans for the future that you are looking forward to? If not what might you like to do. (This should also be discussed in the context of overall life if the person wants to share)		
	What can the company do differently to support you as a person?		
Organisational Morals	What are the Organisational Morals? Lets discuss if they are all still relevant?		
	Choose one moral and discuss how you have been implementing that in the workplace?		
	Choose one moral and discuss how you have been implementing that in the workplace?		

A Culture of Kindness

	What acts of kindness have you been conducting into your life and routine? How does that effect you?		
Energy	What action do you or have you been doing to take care of your overall health/energy levels?		
	What support can we give you in your health?		
	What is your future plan to support your overall health?		
Emotions	How have you been working on with regards to accepting and understanding your emotions?		
	What do you find effects you the most and have you investigated why that is?		
Values	What are your values and your mission statement?		
	Do they still feel relevant?		
	How do you remind yourself of these on a regular basis?		
Your roles	Lets discuss your current roles in life? What are they are?		

A Culture of Kindness

	How do currently manage adapting between the roles?		
Time Management	What tools have you been using to manage your time?		
	What do you think you can do to improve your time management?		
	How do you think you support your team with your time management		
Motivation	What techniques do you use to keep yourself motivated?		
	What could the company and I do to support keeping you motivated?		
Confidence	On a scale of 1-10 how do you feel that your current confidence level is about work and then also for yourself ?		
	What can you do to improve that number if applicable?		
	What can you do to support others in your team with there confidence level?		
Your mental health	What techniques do you use to positively impact your mental health?		

	What can the company put in place to positively impact yours and others mental health?		
Listening skills	What have you learnt recently from really listening to someone?		
	How do you plan to improve your listening this month?		
Their shoes	When did you last use the 'putting yourself in there shoes exercise.		
	What did you learn from that experience		
Acceptance	When have you ensure someone has been included?		
	How do you bring inclusivity and diversity into your day to day work so it becomes embedded without effort?		
Communication Skills	What type of communicator have you been lately, Direct, supportive? How is that working for you?		
	How do you plan to challenge your communication skills over the coming months?		

Influence: persuading others.	How have you had to persuade others lately?		
	What did you learn from that experience?		
Inspirational leadership:	How have you shared your vision with the team.		
	How do help deliver the company vision		
Developing others	Give an example of where you have supported someone else in sharing knowledge, skills or feedback?		
Change catalyst	Where you believe there is a change that is required and why?		
	Discuss how you believe that can happen		
Conflict management	When have you recently settled disputes and difference of opinions lately?		
	What did you learn from that experience?		
Building bonds	How have you been building networks?		
	What have been the challenge that you have overcome with regarding to networking?		
Teamwork and collaboration	How have you been working well in a team recently?		

	What did you learn in that process?		
Gratitude	How do you give gratitude each day		
	Are there other ways you think you might try and what works for you that you would like to share with me or/ and the team.		
Trust	How have you built trust or lost trust with someone lately?		
	What did you learn from that experience?		
Integrity	Where have you been able to demonstrate excellent integrity?		
	What did you learn from that experience?		
Empathy	Where have you demonstrated excellent empathy		
	What did you learn from that experience?		
Time	Give an example of when you have really given someone your time?		
	How did that feel? What did you learn from that experience?		
Connection	When have you worked on a making a connection that didn't work out?		

A Culture of Kindness

	What did you learn from that experience?		
Courage	When did you really test your courage and so something out of your comfort zone?		
	What will you do from now until our next review to challenge your courage		
Reverse Mentoring	What reserve mentoring have you completed this review period		
	What did you learn form that?		
	What will you next review period?		

A Culture of Kindness

References

1. Kjellberg, P. (10 May 2005) Confucianism: Intelligent kindness; *philosophytalk.org*; https://www.philosophytalk.org/blog/confucianism-intelligent-kindness (Retrieved August 2019).

2. DiSalvo, D. (September 2009) Perspectives: Forget Survival of the Fittest: It Is Kindness That Counts. *SA Mind* 20, 5, 18-19. doi:10.1038/scientificamericanmind0909-18.

3. Blackburn, E. & Epel, E. (2017) The Telomere Effect: A revolutionary approach to living younger, healthier, longer. Orion Publishing Group, London.

4. Hamilton, D.R. (12 September 2013) The 5 Side-Effects of kindness. *www.drdavidhamilton.com* https://drdavidhamilton.com/the-5-side-effects-of-kindness-2/ (Retrieved August 2019).

5. Roberts, R. (29 August 1994) True Story: Not in public, please: Behold the unkindness of strangers. *The Independent*. https://www.independent.co.uk/voices/true-story-not-in-public-please-behold-the-unkindness-of-strangers-1386354.html (Retrieved August 2019).

6. Wallace, J. & Thurman, B. (2018) Quantifying Kindness, Public Experience and Place: Experiences of people in the UK and Ireland: Data Booklet. The Carnegie Trust.

7. Coyle, D. (2019) The Culture Code: The secrets of highly successful groups. Random House Business.

8. Kotter, J.P. & Heskett, J.L. (1992). *Corporate Culture and Performance*. New York: Free Press.

9. The Six Seconds Model of EQ. https://www.6seconds.org/2010/01/27/the-six-seconds-eq-model/ (Retrieved August 2019).

10. Ma, V., & Schoeneman, T.J. (1997) Individualism Versus Collectivism: A Comparison of Kenyan and American Self-Concepts. *Basic and Applied Social Psychology*. 19: 261-273.

11. Felps W; Mitchell TR; Byington E (2006), How, When and Why Bad Apples Spoil the Barrel: Negative group members and Dysfunctional Groups. *Research in Organisational behavior*. Vol 27 : 175 - 222

12. Rogers, C. (1959) A Theory of Therapy, Personality and Interpersonal Relationships as Developed in the Client-Centered Framework. In (ed.) S. Koch, *Psychology: A Study of a Science. Vol. 3: Formulations of the Person and the Social Context*. New York: McGraw Hill.

13. Kohlberg, L. (1971) From Is to Ought: How to Commit the Naturalistic Fallacy and Get Away with It in the Study of Moral Development. New York: Academic Press.

14. Gallup World Poll. www.gallup.com/services/170945/world-poll.aspx (Retrieved August 2019).

15. BBC News (24 April 2018) *Myanmar Rohingya: What you need to know about the crisis*. https://www.bbc.co.uk/news/world-asia-41566561. (Retrieved August 2019).

16. Spurlock, M. (2004) *Supersize Me* Samuel Goldwyn Films.

17. Peysakhovich A, Rand, D.G. (2016) Habits of virtue: Creating cultures of cooperation and defection in the laboratory. *Management Science*. 62 631-647.

18. Porath, C. (2016) Mastering Civility: A manifesto in the workplace. Grand Central Publishing.

19. Price, M. (2017) Fairness for All: Unlocking the power of employee engagement, David Fickling Books.

20. Cartwright, R. (21 May 2014). The Future of Leadership is More "Feminine" – KLCM 2014. *Ketchum Leadership Blog.* (https://www.ketchum.com/the-future-of-leadership-communication-is-more-feminine-findings-from-the-2014-klcm/ (Retrieved August 2019).

21. Kiel, F. (2015) Return on Character: The real reason leaders and their companies win. Harvard Business Review Press.

22. Cuddy, A., Kohut, M. & Neffinger, J. (2013) Connect, then lead. *Harvard Business Review.* https://hbr.org/2013/07/connect-then-lead/ar/1 (Retrieved August 2019).

23. Phillips, A. (2013) Missing Out: in Praise of the unlived life. New York: Farrar, Straus and Giroux.

24. Hari, J. (2019) Lost Connections: Why you're depressed and how to find hope. Bloomsbury Publishing.

25. McManus, S., Meltzer, H., Brugha, T. S., Bebbington, P. E., & Jenkins, R. (2009). Adult psychiatric morbidity in England, 2007: results of a household survey. The NHS Information Centre for health and social care.

26. Rosie (21 August 2017). Do you know your Millennials from your Generation X? *Social-Change.org.uk blog.* https://social-change.co.uk/blog/2017-08-21-do-you-know-your-millennials-from-your-generation-x (Retrieved August 2019).

27. Giles, C. (13 August 2018) Britain's Productivity Crisis in Eight Charts. *FT.com.* https://www.ft.com/content/6ada0002-9a57-11e8-9702-5946bae86e6d (Retrieved August 2019).

28. Mental Health Foundation. https://www.mentalhealth.org.uk/a-to-z/p/physical-health-and-mental-health.

29. Sattersfield, J.M. (2015) Cognitive-Behavioral Therapy: Techniques for training your brain. The Great Courses.

30. Six Seconds. *Emotions, Feelings and Moods: Does anybody know the difference?* https://www.6seconds.org/2017/05/15/emotion-feeling-mood/ (Retrieved August 2019).

31. Fleming, J.E. & Kocovski, N.L. (2014) Mindfulness and acceptance-based group therapy for social anxiety disorder: A treatment manual, Second edition. https://www.actonsocialanxiety.com/pdf/magt_for_SAD_2nd_ed.pdf (Retrieved August 2019).

32. Freud, S (1923) *The ego and the id.* SE, 19: 1-66.

33. https://www.mentalhealth.org.uk/a-to-z/p/physical-health-and-mental-health (Retrieved August 2019).

34. Dweck, C. S. (2008). Can personality be changed? Current Directions in Psychological Science, 17(6), 391-394.

35. Type A and Type B Personality Theory (28 July 2019) *Wikipedia.* h t t p s : / / e n . w i k i p e d i a . o r g / w i k i / Type_A_and_Type_B_personality_theory (Retrieved August 2019).

36. Mueller, M., & Dweck, C. S. (1998). Intelligence praise can undermine motivation and performance. Journal of Personality and Social Psychology, 75, 33-52.

37. Treadway, M.T., Buckholz, J.W., Cowan, R.L., Woodward, N.D., Li, R., Sib Ansari. M., Baldwin, R.M., Schwartzman, A.N., Kessler, R.M. & Zald, D.H. (2012) Dopaminergic Mechanisms of Individual Differences in Human Effort-Based Decision-Making. *The Journal of Neuroscience* 32(18).

38. Brown, B. (2012) *Listening to Shame.* TED2012. https://www.ted.com/talks/brene_brown_listening_to_shame?language=en (Retrieved August 2019).

39. Gibran, K. (1923) *The Prophet* 1972: Reprint edition. William Heinemann.

40. Rock, D. (2008) SCARF: A brain-based model for collaborating with and influencing others. *Neuroleadership Journal (1).*

41. Maslow, A.H. (1943). A theory of human motivation. *Psychological Review.* 50 (4): 370–96.

42. Meet-up (https://www.meetup.com).

43. Katz, D. (1964) The motivational basis of organizational behavior. In: *Behavioral science*, 1964.

44. Heath, C. & Heath, D. (2006) The Curse of Knowledge. *Harvard Business Review*. https://hbr.org/2006/12/the-curse-of-knowledge;at/1 (Retrieved August 2019).

45. Horowitz, M. & Whipple Callahan, M. (9 June 2016) How Leaders Inspire: Cracking the code. *Bain & Company Brief*. https://www.bain.com/insights/how-leaders-inspire-cracking-the-code/ (Retrieved August 2019).

46. How to be an Inspirational Leader (3 February 2017) *Bain & Company* https://www.bain.com/insights/how-to-be-an-inspirational-leader-infographic/ (Retrieved August 2019).

47. Flade, P., Asplund, J. & Elliott, G. (8 October 2015) Employees who use their strengths outperform those who don't. *Gallup Workplace*. https://www.gallup.com/workplace/236561/employees-strengths-outperform-don.aspx (Retrieved August 2019)

48. Thompson, J. (17 September 2015) http://www.chicagotribune.com/business/ct-bain-inspirational-leadership-0918-biz-20150917-story.html (Retrieved August 2019).

49. Finney, L. *Inspirational Leadership: Six must-haves to develop inspirational talent within your organisation* Thales Learning & Development White Paper. https://www.apm.org.uk/media/12077/thales-whitepaper_inspirational-leadership.pdf (Retrieved August 2019).

50. Kunz, P. R., & Woolcott, M. (1976). Season's greetings: From my status to yours. *Social Science Research*. 5 (3): 269–278.

A Culture of Kindness

51. Pruyser, P. W. (1976). The minister as diagnostician: Personal problems in pastoral perspective. Philadelphia: Westminster Press. (p69).

52. Harvard Health Publishing (November 2011) In praise of gratitude. *Harvard Mental Health Newsletter* http://www.health.harvard.edu/newsletter_article/in-praise-of-gratitude (Retrieved August 2019).

53. The Greater Good Science Center. (https://ggsc.berkeley.edu/what_we_do/major_initiatives/expanding_gratitude) and (https://www.templeton.org) (Retrieved August 2019).

54. Greenberg, M. S., & Westcott, D. R. (1983). Indebtedness as a mediator of reactions to aid. In J. D. Fisher, A. Nadler, & B. M. DePaulo (Eds.), *New directions in helping: Recipient reactions to aid* (Vol. 1, pp. 85–112). New York: Academic Press.

55. Wong, J. & Brown, J. (6 June 2017). How gratitude changes you and your brain. *Greater Good Magazine*. https://greatergood.berkeley.edu/article/item/how_gratitude_changes_you_and_your_brain (Retrieved May 21, 2019).

56. Bartlett, M.Y., & DeSteno, D. (2006). Gratitude and prosocial behavior: Helping when it costs you. *Psychological Science, 17*(4), 319-325.

57. Huffman, J.C., DuBois, C.M., Healy, B.C., Boehm, J.K., Kashdan, T.B., Celano, C.M., Denninger, J.W., Lyubomirsky, S. (2014). Feasibility and utility of positive psychology exercises for suicidal inpatients. *General Hospital Psychiatry, 36*(1), 88-94.

58. Wood, A. M., Maltby, J., Gillett, R., Linley, A., & Joseph, S. (2008). The role of gratitude in the development of social support, stress, and

depression: Two longitudinal studies. *Journal of Research in Personality, 42*(4), 854-871.

59. Huffman, J.C., Beale, E.E., Beach, S.R., Celano, C.M., Belcher, A.M., Moore, S.V., Suarez, L. Gandhi, P.U., Motiwala, S.R., Gaggin, H., & Januzzi, J.L. (2015). Design and baseline data from the Gratitude Research in Acute Coronary Events (GRACE) study. *Contemporary Clinical Trials, 44*, 11-19.

60. Mills, P.J., Redwine, L., Wilson, K., Pung, M.A., Chinh, K., Greenberg, B.H., Lunde, O., Maisel, A., Raisinghani, A. (2015). The role of gratitude in spiritual well-being in Asymptomatic heart failure patients. *Spirituality in Clinical Practice, 2*(1), p. 5-17.

61. Liang, H., Chen, C., Li, F., Wu, S., Wang, L., Zheng, X., & Zeng, B. (2018). Mediating effects of peace of mind and rumination on the relationship between gratitude and depression among Chinese university students. *Current Psychology, p. 1-8.*

62. Fehr, R., Fulmer, A., Awtrey, E. & Miller, J.A. (2016) The Grateful Workplace: A multilevel model of gratitude in organizations. *Academy of Management Review* 42 (2).

63. Chapman, G. (1990) The Five Love Languages: The secret to love that lasts. Northfield Publishing.

64. Seligman, M., Steen, T.A., Park, N. & Peterson, C. (2005) Positive Psychology Progress: Empirical Validation of Interventions. *American Psychologist* 60(5): 410-21.

65. PWC (2016) *19th Annual Global CEO Survey: Redefining business success in a changing world.* https://www.pwc.com/gx/en/ceo-survey/

2016/landing-page/pwc-19th-annual-global-ceo-survey.pdf (Retrieved August 2019).

66. *Statistics: A matter of trust* (1998) Consultation Document. The Stationery Office. https://assets.publishing.service.gov.uk/government/uploads/system/uploads/attachment_data/file/260823/report.pdf (Retrieved August 2019).

67. Morgan, H. (15 March 2019) *Public Trust in Official Statistics.* NatCen. http://www.natcen.ac.uk/blog/public-trust-in-official-statistics (Retrieved August 2019).

68. Ipsos Mori (30 November 2017) *Trust in Professions: Long-term trends.* https://www.ipsos.com/ipsos-mori/en-uk/trust-professions-long-term-trends (Retrieved August 2019).

69. Arrow, K. (1972) Gifts and Exchanges, *Philosophy and Public Affairs*, (1), 343-362.

70. Edelman (20 January 2019) *2019 Trust Barometer* https://www.edelman.com/trust-barometer (Retrieved August 2019).

71. CitiGroup & LinkedIn (28 October 2014) New Citi/ LinkedIn Survey Reveals Men Struggle with Work/Life Balance - but may not be telling women their concerns. https://www.citigroup.com/citi/news/2014/141028a.htm (Retrieved August 2019).

72. 'Integrity'. *Wikipedia, The Free Encyclopedia.,*22 August 2019) https://en.wikipedia.org/w/index.php?title=Integrity&oldid=912034329. (accessed August 2019).

73. Heathfield, S. (4 February 2019) *What is Integrity – Really?* https://www.thebalancecareers.com/what-is-integrity-really-1917676 (Retrieved August 2019).

74. Scouts News and Blogs (2 October 2018) *Scouts call for action to end UK's 'crisis of empathy.* https://www.scouts.org.uk/news/2018/10/scouts-calls-for-action-to-end-uks-crisis-of-empathy/ (Retrieved August 2019).

75. Wiseman, T. (1996) A concept analysis of empathy. *JAN (Journal of Advanced Nursing)* 23(6).

76. Park, S.Q., Kahnt, T., Dogan, A., Strang, S., Fehr, E. & Tobler, P.N. A neural link between generosity and happiness. *Nature Communications*, 2017; 8: 15964.

77. White, R., Jobe, W. & Dishaw, K. (2014) *Connecting Happiness and Success* Chapter 3: Positive Relationships. https://www.connectinghappinessandsuccess.com/overview/happiness-concepts/3-positive-relationships/. (Retrieved August 2019).

Printed in Poland
by Amazon Fulfillment
Poland Sp. z o.o., Wrocław